# Praise for
# *Talk to Me*

"Kim Bearden is not only a master of words, but a master in the art of relationships. Her ability to weave personal tales, life experience, and practical advice into one book makes this a natural fit for individuals at any stage in life. You will walk away from this book a better communicator, a more compassionate soul, and one who is motivated to make meaningful connections with others."

*—Adam Dovico, principal and author of* Inside the Trenches *and* The Limitless School

"*Talk to Me* provides a brilliant step-by-step guide on how to effectively communicate from the heart. This book is more than a book on communication; it is filled with experience, knowledge, and practical steps on how to build relationships through effective and loving communication. Kim leads by example and as our friend, leader, and colleague, we have always felt more than comfortable to go to her for advice, support, or to simply chat. There is a reason why everyone calls her mom, and this book explains how she uses her gift of giving to create relationships based on honest, loving, and respectful communication. *Talk to Me* is an inspiring and motivating guide that every educator will benefit from."

*—Hope and Wade King, authors of* The Wild Card

"There are a handful of authors that, the moment they release a book, I rush out to buy it. Kim Bearden is one of those authors. As I read *Talk to Me*, I found myself yet again hanging on her every word. I took notes on almost every page and left little markers throughout the book to note ideas that I wanted to re-visit and share with others. Communication, and the how-tos for doing it well, are so needed in our day and age, and Kim's honesty and passion in *Talk to Me* shines brightly. This is a book that every educator (and adult in general) should pick up and learn from immediately."

*—Todd Nesloney, award-winning educator, international speaker, and bestselling author*

"The first time I met Kim Bearden, her warm smile and radiating joy drew me toward her. That first impression led us into having a twenty-minute conversation that gave me the fuel to be the educator I am today. As you read *Talk to Me*, you will feel the same connection I felt. 'Auntie' Kim has broken down the arduous concept of communication through storytelling and vivid examples that provide great clarity. Her book will encourage you to become a better teacher, and most importantly, a better human being."

—*Michael Bonner, second-grade teacher,*
*author of* Get Up or Give Up

"Our words hold power and have the ability to influence others, but so often things get in the way of our intended message. In this insightful, vividly written guide for becoming a master communicator, Kim Bearden once again weaves the magic that draws you in—not only giving us content but also painting a vibrant picture of practicality. *Talk to Me* is an instant must-read for anyone looking to inspire, encourage, and get things done!"

—*James Whitfield, leadership development strategist,*
*The Flippen Group*

"*Talk to Me* should be required reading . . . for everyone! Whether you are a teacher, business professional, community leader, or parent, you will find yourself in the stories and on the pages of Kim Bearden's latest book. Through skillful storytelling, Kim inspires and challenges us to grow as effective, authentic communicators and by doing so helps us to lead lives and careers filled with abiding joy and a strong sense of purpose."

—*Brian Sinchak, president, Lakewood Catholic Academy,*
*Cleveland, Ohio*

"Somehow, with every word she writes, Kim Bearden is able to communicate the passion, heart, and magic that she has always exhibited as an educator and that is needed in every classroom in America. She reminds us all about the art and heart of education."

—*Dr. Billy Snow, superintendent,*
*Cedar Hill Independent School District*

"Even the most seasoned and successful educators fall short in certain areas, and Kim simplifies and details all the areas necessary to not only be a successful educator, but to be a very well-rounded educator. This book is so insightful and focuses on all the core qualities that we all need to connect to our students, and empower, nurture and inspire our students. It reminded me that education is more about inspiration than information; it's more about equity than equality. This book serves as a foundation for new educators and a much-needed reminder for veteran educators."

*—Nick Ferroni, NYC educator and activist*

"Finally! An invaluable, one-of-a-kind resource created for teachers by one of our own! Kim Bearden—perhaps the most dedicated, passionate, talented, loving educators on the planet—has distilled key lessons learned across the span of her incredible career and offers them here in vibrant, engaging format. If you want to inspire, encourage, and get things done, carve out some time to dive into Kim's book, *Talk to Me.*"

*—June Teisan, veteran urban middle school educator,*
*National Teacher Hall of Fame Inductee 2016*

"*Talk to Me* is a window into the miraculous world of Kim Bearden, where meaningful relationships with students and their families catalyze transformative learning and growth. This book is a reminder that education is a people profession and that the best teachers know when to ask, when to tell, and, most importantly of all, when to simply listen. All professionals who are determined to build impact—and who aren't afraid to imagine better versions of themselves—should read *Talk to Me.* Then, they should read it again."

*—Wade Whitehead, award winning educator and speaker, creator*
*of the Teachers of Promise Foundation, National Teacher Hall of*
*Fame Inductee 2016*

"*Talk to Me* is an honest, transparent, and relatable conversation, highlighting intentional communication practices. Kim Bearden has woven a reflective tapestry of essential communication principles, which aim to create a ubiquitous culture of cognizant listeners, speakers, and world-changers. Designed to complement and reinforce one another, each principle empowers and inspires novice and veteran communicators to begin every interaction with a mindful heart of understanding."

—*Stephanie Frosch, communications coordinator*

"Talk to Me is a practical, relatable, and inspiring work by the incomparable Kim Bearden which reminds us all of the power of "what we say and how we say it." Amidst the bustle of life where communications are often reduced to line spaces and curt encounters, Kim drills down to six principles which should drive our oral and written communications as we take on the God-given responsibility of interacting with others in a way that promotes dignity, respect, and love for one another."

—*Mrs. Gina Coss, EdS, principal, Saint Gregory the Great Catholic School, Virginia Beach, Virginia*

# Talk to Me

## Find the Right Words to Inspire, Encourage, and Get Things Done

**6** **Principles of Effective Communication**

## Kim Bearden

*Talk to Me*
© 2018 by Kim Bearden

This book is available at special discounts when purchased in quantity for use as premiums, promotions, fundraisers, or for educational use. For inquiries and details, contact the publisher at books@daveburgessconsulting.com.

Published by Dave Burgess Consulting, Inc. San Diego, California, daveburgessconsulting.com

Cover Design by Genesis Kohler
Cover photo by J. Amezqua
Editing and Interior Design by My Writers' Connection

Library of Congress Control Number: 2018944249
Paperback ISBN: 978-1-946444-85-1
Ebook ISBN: 978-1-946444-86-8
9781949595741
First Printing: July 2018

**DEDICATION**
To my amazing husband, Scotty—you are my rock.

To my precious daughter, Madison—you fill my heart
with abundant joy.

To my beloved sons, Sisipho, Sabelo,
and Phakamani.
You are proof that miracles are real.

# CONTENTS

# FOREWORD

When Kim and I first decided to start a school together, one of our first hurdles was finding a location. We stumbled upon a 100-year-old abandoned factory that was a haven for prostitution and drug activity. It was located in a crime riddled area of the South Atlanta neighborhood, and we instantly said, "This is it!"

While many said our decision was preposterous, Kim and I held steadfast that the transformation we would make to that building would mimic the revolutionary impact we hoped to have on our students and the education profession. Little did we know that there would be many more gargantuan hurdles to come and that the revolution would come with great sacrifices...and bravery. One day, while Kim and I walked the halls of the dilapidated factory, brushing away cobwebs and meandering through clouds of dust, we realized that we weren't alone. We froze in place as we saw long, dark shadows at the end of the hall, and then suddenly two men dressed in dark clothing exited one of the rooms and turned down the hall toward us. They were arguing over something and didn't see us immediately, and it was obvious that no good intentions surrounded their visit to our newly purchased crime haven.

And then I ran. I just ran with all I had in me, through the lobby, out the door and across the street. It wasn't until I was far enough away and bathed in the light of day that I felt secure enough to turn back to make sure the men hadn't followed us. It was then that I realized Kim wasn't with me! She was still inside! In my mind as I ran out of the building I had been "leading by example" and assumed Kim would come with me, but apparently, she didn't get that memo. For some reason I could not fathom, she remained inside the building!

*Crap.* What in the world was I to do? Without thinking, I just darted back to the building, terrified but certain I had to do something to save Kim! Just prior to reaching the front door, Kim coolly walked out and said, "They ran out the back door before I could catch them." My blonde and brilliant superhero friend had actually gone after the trespassers as I ran across the parking lot with arms flailing as if I were actually on fire.

My hero.

My badass friend.

And the genius cofounder of our school.

That wasn't the first time, and it wouldn't be the last, that Kim has come to my rescue, stood strong as my champion, guarded my feelings and saved my life, literally and figuratively. However, her greatest skill and the greatest way she has affected my life doesn't deal with her bravery, her resilience, or her creative acumen. Kim's talent that has contributed the most to my life is her way with words. I've never met a person with a gift to relate to everyone around her, to build bonds with any personality type, and to communicate in such an effective manner as to calm fears, inspire hope, and bring resolution to any conflict.

I first noticed her gift when she and I had the opportunity to present our plan for our school to a room full of business leaders who were potential donors. I went first and gave an impassioned speech where I jumped on a table, leapt from chair to and chair, and demonstrated as much energy as I could muster. Afterward, Kim took the floor, and I watched her completely transform the executives in the room. While I had been a "speaker on crack," she wove a story, meandering through the tables, looking everyone in the eyes, touching their shoulders and connecting with their hearts. When she spoke, it wasn't a speech. It was as if she were having a conversation with an intimate friend. She made everyone feel comfortable and at ease as she connected them with her message and our mission of building a school that would transform the education profession. Kim's masterful command of how to communicate to the people in that room transformed me forever, and I quickly realized just how much I had to learn from my genius friend.

Shortly after we opened RCA, we were meeting with a parent who was furious that we had given her child a detention, causing her to have to bring him to school on Saturday morning. The mother told us that she and the father had recently "split" and that she had to work

Saturday morning and therefore couldn't take him to the detention. Well, our policy at RCA is quite clear, and I explained to the mother that she would have to find a relative to bring him so that he could serve the detention because if we made an exception for him we'd have to make it for everyone. This, of course, didn't solve the problem or go over well, and the mother became more defensive.

And then, Kim slowly reached out, took the mother's hand and said in her calm and reassuring way, "Mama, I can only imagine how difficult this has been for you. You are having to deal with so much right now, and we want to help you during this time."

Kim accurately realized that the mom's anger wasn't toward us; it was directed at her husband who had left the family. She has such an incredible gift for seeing beyond a person's words and realizing their true feelings and intentions.

Suddenly, the mom's demeanor changed, and Kim said, "How can we help you?" and instantly the mom put her head down and started to cry.

Kim consoled the mom, and we both put our arms around her and let her cry. It was obvious she needed to have that release, and once she gained her composure, she said, "You already do so much for me and my child. I was embarrassed that I didn't have anyone to take him to detention on Saturday and I was afraid you were going to think I'm a bad mom. I'm just doing the best I can."

That next hour I watched brilliance in action as Kim soothed, encouraged and uplifted that mother. Her choice of words, her astute understanding of the situation and her genuine desire to show love and help the mother were all more impressive than any communication between two people that I had ever seen. Kim and I cofounded our school together, but I realized that in many ways I was going to be a student of hers as well. The knowledge Kim has to share about how to talk to people, how to get others to understand one's perspective, and how to bring a group of random people to a harmonious consensus are essential skills that can help us all be more successful in both our personal and professional lives.

For years, I have begged Kim to write this book. She teaches all day, trains thousands of educators a year, serves as the executive director of one of the most innovative and dynamic schools in the world, makes speeches for corporations and school districts across the country, and raises her four beautiful children with her husband Scotty. Her life is so full, and she has often said, "I'll get to it!" She's so selfless and she is always using her time to help others, but I finally said, "Kim, writing this book for others is the greatest gift you can give to us all." We all *need* this book more than we probably even realize. So, when I heard Kim say, "Guess what? I finished it," I rejoiced!

We live in a world where many geniuses and masters of their crafts never truly share their knowledge and talents with the world. Thankfully, this isn't one of those times. Within this book, Kim has laid out her secrets for effective communication for all of us, and by experiencing this book you'll be opening yourself up to a transformation that could profoundly change your life. I've had the privilege of having Kim as a best friend and a "life guide" for many years. I'd have the honor of having her "talk to me" in the times I needed her the most. Now, it's your turn to experience her brilliance. It's your time to have her there for you when you need her the most. Great success in life and work is on the way! Good luck on the journey!

*–Ron Clark*

# PREFACE

The percussion of hammering, drilling, and sawing reverberated off the old brick walls, permeating the Sentence Construction Zone. Wide-eyed, my students tiptoed through scaffolding, caution tape, and sawhorses as they scurried to don their hardhats and safety vests. Multicolored lengths of lumber filled their workspaces, each color representing different kinds of clauses and conjunctions.

The students built "paragraph walls" using various patterns of lumber blocks that represented different types of clauses and conjunctions. As they worked, they realized the objective of the lesson: Their well-written paragraphs contained many different sentence patterns, thus creating more colorful, interesting structures. Their weaker paragraphs lacked variety and depth, like a building with no foundation. Resolved to have the best walls possible, many asked if they could revise their work.

As we analyzed what we had learned, Mekhi asked, "Mrs. Bearden, this helps us understand the sentence structure, but what about the content of the sentences? That is important, too, right?"

"Absolutely! You have just provided the perfect segue to my next point. Today we were looking at the structure of your words, but if your content is weak, your walls will still collapse! Content is always the most important thing; the blocks are just tools to help you convey it."

As I packed away the blocks that afternoon, my mind leapt to the concept of this book. For quite a while, I had wanted to write a book about the importance of effective communication, but I needed to find the words to explain exactly how I do what I do. And then it hit me: Our ability to communicate with one another is often like those paragraph walls. The words we use and choose are vitally important, but sometimes, we need to know how to put the building blocks together to build a solid foundation that will hold up well—even when conflict tries to shake it.

I lack a number of talents: I can't dance, I can't draw, and my cooking abilities leave a lot to be desired. But I have been told I have a way with words when interacting with people, even in the most challenging of situations. After my *aha!* moment with the lumber blocks, I realized that, through years of experience, I had developed the use of certain "building blocks"—principles—that I apply to my daily interactions with others. These principles came so naturally that I hadn't reflected upon them before, but once I sat down to analyze my communication style and the communication styles of leaders I admire, I realized that these principles could be easily taught to others, and I have been doing so ever since.

In my first book, *Crash Course: The Life Lessons My Students Taught Me*, I shared stories of my classroom adventures and the lessons that I learned from my interactions with the amazing children in my life. It was my prayer that my words inspired and uplifted teachers while simultaneously giving them strategies to use to improve their classroom instruction and their relationships with students.

Our relationships with our students should always be the priority, but our relationships with our coworkers, parents, and community members also play a vital role in the drama of an educator's life. Discord among these stakeholders can be enough to make a teacher quit the profession, even when that teacher still loves being in the classroom. The same holds true for other careers as well. No matter where you work, dealing with people is often one of the most stressful parts of the job.

During the past thirty-one years, I have served as a teacher, professional-development trainer, curriculum director, middle school principal, and school board member. I have taught more than three thousand students and have visited schools in forty-six states and on six continents. I am currently the cofounder and executive director of the Ron Clark Academy (RCA), an innovative middle school and educator training facility in Atlanta. I also teach fifth- and sixth-grade language arts each day. In the past eleven years, more than fifty thousand educators have visited our school to observe our classrooms and attend workshops. In other words, I have been fortunate to see and experience quite a bit in my career as an educator.

By sharing the successes, mistakes, and lessons learned along my journey, I hope to equip you with principles that will serve as tools to help you build a better foundation for effective communication. It is my fervent prayer that you will learn how to weave your words in a way that will uplift, inspire, support, inform, transform, and spread kindness to a broken world in desperate need of more love and understanding.

# Part 1
# The Foundation

The six principles serve as the foundational tools to help you build more effective communication. In this section, you will gain an understanding of the principles and the ways to implement them in your daily interactions. The principles are taught in a specific order, for the concepts build upon one another; however, once you have mastered each, you do not have to implement them sequentially. To help you reflect as you learn, each chapter is followed by a summary and suggestions for implementation.

# 1 Consideration

"If you can learn a simple trick, Scout, you'll get along a lot better with all kinds of folks. You never really understand a person until you consider things from his point of view, until you climb inside of his skin and walk around in it."

*—Atticus Finch in* To Kill A Mockingbird *by Harper Lee*

# 2 Motivation

# 3 Appreciation

# 4 Validation

# 5 Conversation

# 6 Celebration

# Consideration

I was engaged in teaching my fifth-grade students a lively song on verb conjugation when I noticed one of my teachers peeking in my door with a look of distress on her face. When she saw my class was in session, she quickly turned and left, so I went looking for her as soon as I dismissed my students. I found her sitting alone in her room, tears pooling in her eyes.

"Do you need me? Are you okay?" I asked.

She did not answer at first; instead, she turned her computer screen toward me and pointed at an email—an email written in capital letters and filled with exclamation points. As I began to read, she exclaimed, "Why on earth is Mrs. Caldwell* so angry? I don't understand. Please scroll down and read what I wrote first. Did I do something wrong?"

The teacher had politely asked for an overdue field-trip permission form, yet somehow the teacher's simple request had angered Mrs. Caldwell. The response was the kind that felt like a punch in the stomach. I didn't get it either. Normally, I encourage teachers to reach out to a parent first before I intercede in a situation, but in this case, this mama's response was not rational. I knew it was my job to contact her instead.

I called and left two voicemail messages that went unreturned. Luckily for me, Mrs. Caldwell picked her daughter up from school

---

*Identifying features and names in the stories I'll share have been changed to protect the privacy of those involved.

each afternoon, so I knew that I could catch her in the carpool line. As I approached her car, Mrs. Caldwell pretended not to see me. She slumped down in her seat, attempting to avoid eye contact. I gently tapped on her window, and she rolled it down, feigning a look of surprise. "Mrs. Bearden . . . uh, hi."

"Hi, Mrs. Caldwell. I am not sure if you received my calls, but I need to talk with you for just a couple of minutes. Don't worry—your daughter is okay. Would you mind parking your car and coming inside?"

As she walked with me into the building, I did everything I could to make small talk, but she wasn't having it. She remained cold and noncommunicative; she walked so slowly to avoid our conversation that I felt like I was walking backward instead of forward just to keep her beside me.

As soon as we sat down in my classroom, I reached across the table, took her hand in mine, and said, "Thank you for taking time to come inside. I know you are probably ready to get home. Is everything all right? Are you okay?"

"What do you mean, am I okay?" she snapped.

"I just wanted to know if you are okay. I care very much about you. Talk to me."

She put her head down and sighed. And then the tears flowed. For the next twenty-six minutes, I said nothing. Not one word. I just nodded and listened as she sobbed about her current situation. In the past two weeks, she had lost her job managing rental properties, thus also losing her rent-free housing on one of the sites. When her husband realized she had lost the job (and their home), he left her. She was driving her sister's car that day because her own car had been repossessed. She finally shouted, "I have lost my job, my car, my husband, and my home, but I am not a bad mother! I am not!"

And just like that, it all made sense. She had equated a teacher reminding her that she had forgotten to turn in a permission form to an accusation of her being a bad mom. Now that is a big leap that seems irrational, but this woman was on the edge. Overwhelmed.

Broken. Done. Her reaction to that friendly reminder had absolutely nothing to do with her daughter's teacher or with me.

She slumped her shoulders, and her sobs quieted into soft weeping. I handed her another tissue, reached for her hand again, and waited. When she raised her head, she said, "Oh, no. I did something terrible. My email was so awful. I need to go apologize right now!"

I finally spoke. "Hold on. First, I want to thank you for entrusting me with all of this. We care about you. I care about you. Life is giving you a lot to deal with all at once, and I am so sorry that you are going through this."

"But I need to go apologize! I feel so terrible!" she repeated, shaking her head.

"Mrs. Caldwell, I don't want you to feel terrible; however, I ask that you never write an email to one of my teachers like that again, and an apology would be nice. When you are struggling, you don't have to share your personal business with us, but if you tell us you are having a tough time, we are here to help in any way that we can." She stood and hugged me tightly for several moments. She thanked me profusely for understanding, and then she hugged me again before leaving. Mrs. Caldwell apologized to the teacher, and she even sent cupcakes to school with her daughter the next morning.

## WE ALL HAVE A STORY

We encounter Mrs. Caldwells every day. They are the overwhelmed, the broken, the lost, the hurt, the scared, and the scarred. And we usually do not have the benefit of knowing their true stories. We brush off such people as crazy or mean, and we let their words and actions steal our joy and break us.

After thirty-one years as an educator, I have dealt with thousands of adults and children, and I have learned that the Mrs. Caldwells feel invisible, and sometimes they shout because they are so desperate to be heard by someone—anyone. Sometimes their pain comes out as insults; sometimes their pain is shown through multiple emailed exclamation points.

Every person on this planet has a story, and it is still being written. Some are living in their brightest chapters; others are in the darkest ones, barely able to turn the page. Realize that others have burdens and pains that we may know nothing about, and these could be framing their comments and reactions and inhibiting their ability to communicate with others appropriately.

When faced with people who seem irrational, consider the fact that you don't know their stories, and remember that there can be a difference

> Realize that others have burdens and pains that we may know nothing about, and these could be framing their comments and reactions and inhibiting their ability to communicate with others appropriately.

between being right and doing the right thing. I had documentation to prove that my teacher was right. The parent was wrong in the way she had responded, and I do not think that we should go through life allowing people to treat us harshly or bully us. But the right thing for me to do in that situation was to listen and to show genuine concern. In doing so, I supported my teacher and made it clear to Mrs. Caldwell that her actions were not acceptable.

In my encounter with Mrs. Caldwell, I followed the six foundational principles that foster effective communication:

*Consideration:* What could be the other party's perspective?

*Motivation:* What is driving the outcomes that I really want from our conversation?

*Appreciation:* What am I grateful for in this situation?

*Validation:* How can I make the other party feel respected and heard?

*Conversation:* What needs to be said? What needs to be heard?

*Celebration:* How can we express our success at reaching understanding?

These principles can be taught to anyone, and I will teach them to you in the pages that follow. They will increase your ability to develop rapport, gain respect, support others, engage listeners, develop insight, be heard, and increase productivity. But—there is a catch. The extent to which these will work will be directly proportional to how much you embrace the importance of the first principle and overarching concept: consideration.

Mrs. Caldwell went from furious to appreciative in one meeting because she believed me when I said I cared. She believed me when I said we were there to help. She believed me because it was true. No matter how planned or eloquent the words you speak may be, at the heart of it all, true leaders understand that communication isn't as much about the words you say as it is about the sincerity with which you say them. Effective communicators understand the idea that, "There is a point to my life, and I am not it." To do the same, we must always consider that there is more to the story, and we must lead with empathy.

> True leaders understand that communication isn't as much about the words you say as it is about the sincerity with which you say them.

Empathy and sympathy are often confused. To put it simply, empathy is the attempt to put yourself in another's shoes—to seek to understand another's perspective. Sympathy is feeling sorry for someone else's circumstances. Now in Mrs. Caldwell's case, I certainly did feel sympathy when I learned what was going on, but before that, I had empathy. Sometimes empathy will lead you to sympathy. Sometimes it will not; however, it will always lead you to a better understanding.

As I walked out to meet her in the pick-up line that day, these were the kinds of thoughts that were going through my mind:

*I wonder what could have triggered that email? Something is obviously going on that I don't understand.*

*Is she going through some type of personal crisis? Could we have done something else that upset her, and is she just responding to suppressed anger about it now?*

*If she is experiencing some type of problem, how can I let her know that we care?*

*I need to figure out how to fix this for the sake of her daughter, the teacher, and the parent.*

Notice how such thoughts are very different than this kind of thinking:

*Who does she think she is?*

*I am going to let her know that I saw that email, and I am not happy!*

*She cannot get away with acting like that! Not on my watch!*

*I have done so much for her child. How dare she! How ungrateful of her!*

*Jeez! This is why I hate my job sometimes! If people only knew what I have to put up with every day!*

You get the picture. Look, I have had those kinds of thoughts, too. But I have learned that consideration for the other person's perspective always leads to better communication. When you learn to see the world this way, you have more peace. Rude comments or actions don't sting nearly as much if you are able to accept that unkind words or deeds might not have anything to do with you at all. Consideration empowers you to be better able to keep your calm. Notice how the first thoughts showed empathy for the parent's perspective. The second set of thoughts was all about my anger, my ego, my frustration, my feelings—me. Choosing to have consideration for Mrs. Caldwell's perspective shaped my approach, softened my tone, and led to a successful outcome.

## SECRET STRUGGLES

Throughout my career, I have learned that when a child is struggling or acting out, there is almost always more to the story. The same holds true for adults. Sometimes we have the benefit to learn what causes people to behave the way that they do. Other times we just have to consider and accept that there could be factors that we will never know.

**Consider Joshua:** Joshua's grades were failing. He was clever, witty, and highly intelligent, yet it seemed that his teachers were putting forth much more effort than he was in school. Joshua continued to have poor work completion and scored abysmally on tests. His teachers grew increasingly frustrated with him; they perceived him to be lazy and ungrateful.

Over the winter break, I noticed a post that he put on social media; it simply read, "I am so hungry." Now, as the mom of three teenage boys, I could argue that teenage boys are always hungry, but in my gut, I felt there was more to the story.

I drove over to Joshua's house to find him there alone with very little food in the pantry. The power was off, and it had been for days. I used my phone to call his mom, and I asked her if I could take Joshua to lunch. Before I hung up, I walked out of the room so I could talk to her privately. "How I can help?" I asked.

Joshua's mom worked hard, but her minimum-wage job made it difficult for her to pay every bill on time, and she often had to choose which ones to let slip. Then the late fees would stack up, making it even harder to catch up. She made sure that her son had a working phone when she was gone so that he could call her in an emergency, but the power bill had been just too much to carry that month. I reassured her that I would help her find some resources to get her back on track.

While Joshua and I chatted over pizza, he said, "Thank you, Mrs. Bearden. I was some kinda hungry! I have been eating lots of ramen noodles, but I couldn't cook them without power."

"Oh, Joshua, I am so sorry. I am going to find your mom some help. Is the power an issue a lot?"

"Yes, ma'am. It isn't a big deal unless I have a lot of homework. Sometimes I try to do it with the flashlight on my phone, but then my phone goes dead, and I have to go sit in the car to charge it again. But my mom won't let me sit out there for long because it is bad on the battery and uses gas."

Yes, Joshua had poor work completion and wasn't studying for tests, but can you understand why? His mother was a devoted, wonderful woman who was doing the best she could to provide for her son. She just couldn't get ahead, despite her efforts.

**Consider Melton:** Melton was often disruptive in class. He would talk out of turn and distract other students. Sometimes he behaved far worse. He would call students names. He would huff and puff disrespectfully when corrected. But you see, just the year before, his abusive father had died of alcoholism. Melton and his mother were left in tremendous debt after paying the funeral expenses, and his confusion over his mixed feelings for his father left him feeling lost. He hated the man who had abused his mother and him and had drunk himself to death, yet Melton's heart yearned for his father, and he still loved him, too. It was all too much, so he was angry because he had a hole in his heart and didn't know how to process the pain.

**Consider Katrina:** Katrina was wealthy, pretty, and smart. Her parents were successful lawyers, and her older brother was studying at an Ivy League school. Katrina lived in a beautiful home and wore only the best clothes that money could buy. Katrina could not make anything less than an "A" or she would be punished. If she didn't excel on the competition cheer squad, her mother would berate her for hours. If she gained a few pounds, her mother told her she wouldn't buy her clothes in "fat" sizes. Katrina had a secret. She felt the pressure to be perfect every day of her life—her parents would accept nothing less. At night when everyone went to sleep, Katrina would binge on food until she could eat no more, and then she would throw up. When she started falling asleep in class, her teachers wondered why. Her eating disorder had begun to control her life.

**Consider Abby:** Abby was promiscuous at a very young age. Her beautiful eyes were barely visible beneath her dark eyeliner, and her clothes always pushed the boundaries of the school dress code. Abby thrived on the attention that the boys gave her, and she pretended she didn't care what others said about her even though I knew that deep inside, she did. Abby's father walked out when she was five years old, and after he left, her mother had brought home a stream of men— men who treated women horribly. Abby yearned to be loved by her father, but he had never contacted her since the day he had departed years before. She longed to be told that she was pretty and smart and special, and so when a boy came along who said the words she was desperate to hear, she gave herself to him, thus giving away a part of her young soul.

**Consider Mrs. Meady:** Mrs. Meady was known as the most negative teacher on staff. Her dour expression was permanently etched into her face, and her cold demeanor made her seem unapproachable. I worked hard to develop a rapport with Mrs. Meady, and one day she disclosed the source of her sorrow: Both her son and her husband had died several years before in a tragic accident. She had once been happy and had loved them both so very much. Losing them was more than she could bear, and she had never recovered from the pain.

I could write a whole book of nothing but stories like these, for these are just some of the children and adults whom I have known and loved during my lifetime. In every one of these scenarios, others had no idea what was really happening, and the individuals or their actions were misinterpreted or misunderstood.

Also consider that even if someone is not going through life-altering circumstances, the day-to-day grind can wear out even the nicest of people. If you overslept this morning, spilled your coffee on your lap while driving, got stuck in traffic, and then arrived at work and realized you left your computer at home, I bet you might be a less-than-cheerful version of yourself. A bad day can leave any of us snappy, weepy, or downright grumpy, and we have to consider that everyone has bad days now and then.

## CONSIDERATION WITH EXPECTATIONS

Consideration does not mean that you allow others to mistreat or bully you. It does not mean that you let others off the hook for bad behavior. It doesn't mean that you make excuses for others or treat them with pity. Consideration means that you continuously strive to seek understanding, and you let that understanding guide the way that you approach your interactions.

> Consideration means that you continuously strive to seek understanding.

Having consideration for what people are going through does not mean you lower your expectations. When you have low expectations, you are really saying, "Darlin', I don't think you can do it, either." High expectations are the outward manifestation of your belief and hope in others, and they are often just what is needed to show that you see greatness within them.

Tobias was a charismatic young man, but over the course of the school year, I watched his grades and his behavior deteriorate. I sat with Tobias, and we talked about

> High expectations are the outward manifestation of your belief and hope in others.

ways to help him succeed in school. Through a series of events, I learned that his mother was bipolar, and her fluctuating moods had begun to grow in intensity. In addition, several extended family members had moved in with them after suffering job losses and other setbacks. The clutter, clamor, and sadness of Tobias's house left him with little motivation to work hard. I showed Tobias empathy, and I offered a number of actions that might help. Unfortunately, he didn't take me up on the opportunities for extra support. I was disappointed, but I knew Tobias was a phenomenal athlete, so I decided that maybe I needed to change my approach and appeal to his competitive side.

During lunch, I pulled Tobias into my office. Tenderly, I said, "Tobias, I wish so much for you. In a perfect world, your sweet mother would be well. You wouldn't have to worry about finances, and your family members would be in a better situation. In a perfect world, your house would be spacious and calm, and you would have a clutter-free place where you could sit and do your work each night; however, this world is not perfect. I so wish it were, but it will never be. I do not pretend to know how hard it is for you—I cannot imagine. But I do know that every one of us has challenges to overcome at some point. Your time is now. And here is the good news, Tobias: You are smart and talented, and I believe that you can do anything you set your mind to. I believe you are strong and you can overcome any obstacles you face."

His eyes pooled with tears, and he swallowed. "Yes, Mrs. Bearden. I am an overcomer. I can do this."

"Yes, sweetie, you can, and I am here to help you do it. You are not alone."

Through continued support coupled with high expectations, Tobias pulled up his grades, and he is now attending college on scholarship. And you would love to hire someone just like him because he is tough and has grit; he is an overcomer. I took all of Tobias's challenges into consideration when communicating with him, and it took an investment of time and several conversations to get him on track. In his case, balancing empathy with high expectations made all the difference.

## THE BENEFIT OF LIFE'S EXPERIENCES

How do you develop the consideration mindset? To truly be empathetic, you have to realize that you simply do not know everything there is to know. Reflect on your own experiences to help you better imagine what life might look like from another's perspective. Think about times in your life where you felt and thought, "If only others knew what I am going through! No one seems to understand me right now."

Here is the CliffsNotes® version of my life: I had a beautiful childhood and upbringing that was followed by marriage, motherhood, betrayal, devastation, divorce, and single parenting my little girl, all while working as an educator. I endured financial ruin—I know what it is to come home to find the lights cut off and the bank account overdrawn. I know what it is to feel crippling self-doubt and overwhelming despair. I eventually experienced true love, a beautiful second marriage, forgiveness, and restoration. I watched my phenomenal daughter grow into a magnificent young woman after enduring her tumultuous teenage years. And I have experienced the joy and challenges that come with adopting three magnificent sons from South Africa. I know what it is to sit at the table with my sons for hours at night after working all day because they had been denied educational access and resources for the first eleven years of their lives.

From parenting four children and teaching thousands more, I know that every child—every person—learns differently, loves differently, and receives discipline differently. I know what it is to be a blended, racially mixed family. I know what it is to watch a parent suffer with Alzheimer's and Parkinson's and that grief comes in waves. I know what it is to love what I do every day. I know what it is to build something from nothing, what it is to lead, and what it is to follow. I know what it feels like to be exhausted beyond measure. I understand how parents can be incensed beyond rational thinking because their love for their children blinds them. I understand how someone can take out anger on the first available target, even though it is misdirected and wrong to do. These are just some of the experiences I draw upon when trying to see—truly see—others.

And despite what I do know, I must also accept that there are so many things that I don't fully understand. I have been blessed with good health and a sound mind. I have never been without a job. I cannot imagine the agony of losing a child. I do not know what it is to be a male. And even though I have three African sons and teach at a school predominately composed of black children, I will never know what it is to be a person of color and both the pride and the pain that being another race can evoke.

Consideration can be extremely challenging when someone sees the world with a completely different lens than you do. But try to realize that in some instances, people have limited perspectives because they have only been exposed to certain ideas and experiences. And the opposite is true, too. Perhaps another's viewpoint is different than yours because that individual has been exposed to and has experienced far more than you have.

> But try to realize that in some instances, people have limited perspectives because they have only been exposed to certain ideas and experiences.

## THE MOST POWERFUL PRINCIPLE

Social media bombards us daily with images of perfection—perfect husbands with perfect wives and perfect children who succeed at every activity and who make stellar grades. We see perfect mothers who never go through the McDonald's drive-thru, who always have clean houses, and who throw dinner parties that belong on Pinterest. Guess what? Perfection is an illusion, and sometimes those who appear to have the most fabulous lives are actually among those who are hurting the most. You never know what is going on behind closed doors. You can never assume someone has an easy go of life, no matter what image that person projects.

> You can never assume someone has an easy go of life, no matter what image that person projects.

And so, I seek to consider and understand all of this with every interaction. I believe consideration is the single greatest factor that has led to my ability to lead and love with success.

What is your story? How can your life experiences and the obstacles you've faced help you realize how others might be thinking and feeling? And if you are one of the few who has led a completely charmed life that has been devoid of pain, how can you read about, learn about, observe, support, and listen to those who have walked a different path so that you can gain some perspective?

When you learn to use the principle of consideration, you will be better able to read between the lines. You will find that you are more perceptive to people's words and actions, even their body language. You will intuitively know when others say, "I'm fine," and they really are not. You will find that you take the time to listen to and care for people. When someone is drowning, you will be moved to offer help; when someone is hurting, you will be inspired to give support.

Surely someone reading this is thinking, "Yeah, that sounds really noble, but what about me? I refuse to be a doormat. If I don't look out for myself, no one else will! What about self-love?" In this day and age where we are often driven by followers and likes, it can be hard to see that considering others first can sometimes be more important than considering ourselves.

Here is a wonderful consequence of living by this principle: When you affect the life of one person, you do not just affect that individual. Your influence can also have an impact upon that person's spouse, children, extended family members, friends, neighbors, colleagues, employees, community members—every person whom that individual influences can indirectly be affected by you. Your impact could reach into hundreds, thousands, or even millions of people's lives. They are people whose names you will never know and whose stories you will never hear, but rest assured knowing that your influence has been divinely woven into their journey. There is no doubt about it: Putting others first gives your life purpose.

Since learning to think and live this way, I am happier. I accomplish more. I feel respected, loved, and appreciated. I have been far more successful at communicating with others, and I go to sleep at night with the reassurance that I live life with purpose, and that feels good. Really, really good.

## CHAPTER SUMMARY

- Every person has a story that is still being written, and some are in the darkest pages of their lives.
- When we take time to consider and empathize with another's possible circumstances or perspective, it enables us to communicate and interact more effectively.
- Showing consideration does not mean that we make excuses for others; high expectations are still important.
- When we uplift others, our lives are redefined as more powerful and significant.
- Considering others' perspectives first can lead to greater understanding, happiness, and success.

## IMPLEMENTATION

The next time you are faced with a difficult conversation, be honest with yourself about your self-centered thoughts and feelings. Jot them down, and then try to reframe them by replacing self-directed emotions with empathetic feelings that take the other person's perspective into consideration.

# 1 Consideration

# 2 Motivation

"A good head and good heart are always a formidable combination."

—Nelson Mandela

# 3 Appreciation

# 4 Validation

# 5 Conversation

# 6 Celebration

# Motivation

After just six years of teaching, I was given a sought-after position as an instructional lead teacher at a high-achieving school. The role required me to provide professional development, conduct model lessons, and meet with parents and educators to determine strategies for meeting the needs of struggling students. I was honored, determined, and absolutely terrified. To make matters even more challenging, a more experienced teacher on staff had applied for the position and was not at all happy that I had been given the job. I was the new girl at a new school, and I felt the need to prove myself and to show everyone that, although I was a mere twenty-seven years old, I knew what I was doing. Within a couple of weeks, I felt like I had the perfect opportunity: a parent-teacher conference for Bradley Halloran, one of our most challenging students. I would take control, provide guidance and solutions, and fix the problems that the parents and teachers were having with him. I was on it!

As Bradley's mother and father entered the conference room, they nodded in acknowledgment, but they did not return my pleasantries. It was obvious that they did not want to be there; they had endured many parent-teacher conferences. Mr. Halloran was a good six feet, four inches tall, and when he sat down, his outstretched legs bumped into mine underneath the table. He did not retract them; rather, he let it be known that the space was his and that I should be the one to move. He further asserted his dominance by folding his arms, leaning back, and squinting at me as though he was sizing me up and trying to determine what on earth qualified me to be there. Mrs. Halloran hugged her purse and looked at the ground. The two teachers who were in attendance repeatedly shuffled their papers, waiting for me to start the conference.

I cleared my throat and nervously began my presentation. I will spare you the details, but it began with my assessment of their child's problems, what they should do about them, and how they needed to design homework time to be more effective. After my arrogant and somewhat ignorant ramblings, I presented them with a contract outlining the responsibilities that the teachers, the parents, and Bradley needed to fulfill in order to help him achieve success.

That conference took place in the fall of 1993, and I still feel the heat of embarrassment rising up my neck as I recall the events. I can remember where I was sitting, what posters lined the walls, and even what I was wearing. I would love to block it all out, and I can barely stand to type it. But I must take responsibility for it. Let me just cut to the chase: It did not go well. At all. Mr. Halloran rolled his eyes and laughed at my suggestions. When I finally stopped talking long enough to listen, he told me all the strategies they had already done, many of which I had not even suggested. He shared some trauma that their son had endured. He expressed his disdain for the lack of understanding I had shown. And he was right.

I made many mistakes that day that made effective communication difficult, but the biggest one was that I began the whole event with the wrong *motivation*:

*I will prove that I am competent and should have this job.*

*I will show them that I am in charge.*

*I will impress them with my organization, suggestions, and solutions.*

Boy, did I miss the mark. I didn't accomplish anything; in fact, I did far more harm than good. If I were in the same situation today, this would be my motivation:

*This boy needs help.*

*The teachers need solutions.*

*The parents need support.*

*I need to listen, learn, and seek to understand what is really going on so that I can help them all.*

Now, is there anything wrong with wanting to please your boss and coworkers? Absolutely not. Your true motivation, however, should be to do your job well to help your colleagues, your students, your clients, or your organization. If the motivation is just to be liked or to impress everyone, you risk the danger of behaving like an insincere suck-up. And people see right through that. People value those who do an exemplary job of serving others, not themselves. The recognition and appreciation you long for will be more meaningful and genuine if you receive it for being a true asset to others and your organization.

Take a look at the list that follows. Are there times when some of these factors are the drivers behind your more challenging communications?

## NEGATIVE MOTIVATORS

| | |
|---|---|
| Anger | Insecurity |
| Attention | Jealousy |
| Control | Lust |
| Defensiveness | Manipulation |
| Ego | Negativity |
| Fear | Power |
| Frustration | Revenge |
| Greed | Self-centeredness |
| Guilt | Self-pity |
| Hatred | Sloth |
| Ignorance | Suspicion |

If any of these traits or emotions drive your behavior, I encourage you to strive to reframe your motivation. Recognizing your thought processes and feelings is the first step.

What would your interactions with others be like if the following positive emotions and traits drove your motivation instead?

## POSITIVE MOTIVATORS

| | |
|---|---|
| Compassion | Patience |
| Dedication | Peace |
| Determination | Persistence |
| Diligence | Positivity |
| Empathy | Productivity |
| Engagement | Resolution |
| Gentleness | Service |
| Goodness | Significance |
| Grit | Solutions |
| Insight | Support |
| Joy | Truth |
| Kindness | Understanding |
| Knowledge | Wisdom |
| Love | |

Would you rather work with someone who operates from the negative or the positive motivators? Which kind of person would you rather have as your boss? Whom would you trust? Whom would you befriend? Marry?

Be that person.

As you live, move, breathe, and speak, your motives behind your everyday interactions affect the way others perceive you and trust you. Regardless

> Your motives behind your everyday interactions affect the way others perceive you and trust you.

of whether they are positive or negative, your motives have an impact upon your ability to communicate effectively to achieve your desired outcome. For example, the negative motivators of insecurity, ego, and desire for control affected my conference with the Hallorans—and Mr. Halloran saw right through me. He responded with utter disdain for me, and I lost respect rather than gained it. But with Mrs. Caldwell, my motivation was to help her, her child, and the teacher. And I succeeded. My motivation framed and influenced my approach and the words I chose, and she felt cared for and heard as a result.

Unless you are a master manipulator, perceptive people can read your motives. You know that feeling of unease you get with some people? That voice inside your head that gives you pause? You know those times when you can't put your finger on the reason, but you feel a lack of trust? That inner voice is your intuition letting you know that although the person might be saying all the right words, the motive behind them is not honorable.

Before we hire a teacher to work at RCA, the candidate must spend the day with us and teach a model lesson. Several years ago, we were really excited about an accomplished teacher applicant who had just about every credential possible. This teacher was an award-winning educator, and she taught a solid lesson to our students and effectively utilized research-based practices.

She was completely shocked when we didn't hire her.

She had all the right degrees and skills, but her motives weren't a fit for our school. This teacher spent the whole day in our classrooms, but she couldn't give me the name of a single child. I admire confident women, but she was quick to tout her awards and take all the credit for her success. She talked negatively about her coworkers, and her arrogance was off-putting. During her interview, our entire committee felt like she wanted to be a part of our team simply to add clout to her résumé. Her motivation wasn't to help our students or other educators; our intuition told us that it was to promote herself.

## DO THE RIGHT THINGS FOR THE RIGHT REASONS

If you have the wrong motives, even the good things you do don't work out as well as they would have if you had done them for noble reasons. Tutoring a student, for example, is a good thing. But if you only do it to please your boss or to play the martyr, others will eventually question your motives, especially your students. If, on the other hand, you provide extra help to students because you care about them and want to help them succeed, your sincerity will create a genuine bond that will serve as a foundation for a more meaningful flow of communication.

> If you have the wrong motives, even the good things you do don't work out as well as they would have if you had done them for noble reasons.

Are you conflicted about where your motives lie? Here is a challenge for you: Do an extravagant act of kindness, but do it without touting it, posting it, or seeking credit for it. The concept of random acts of kindness is a beautiful one, but I also like to intentionally choose people who I know need support or encouragement. Buy someone groceries. Spend time with someone who is lonely. Go out of your way to lend a helping hand to an overwhelmed coworker. Clean someone's house, babysit for someone who needs a break, wash someone's car, or organize someone's office or garage. Write letters telling others what you see in them, just because.

For years, I have made an effort to do extravagant acts of kindness to keep myself focused on pure motives. I won't share the things I have done here; that would defeat the whole purpose by drawing attention to myself. But I encourage you to try it even if you secretly wish someone would do one for you. Even if you are struggling, pour your energy into brightening someone else's world. Do something amazing and completely out of the ordinary, and don't tell anybody. You will want to so badly, but make that kindness your secret. Your soul will be rewarded immeasurably. I guarantee it.

> Do something amazing and completely out of the ordinary, and don't tell anybody.

## CHAPTER SUMMARY

- The motivation behind our interactions influences our outcomes.
- Selfish motivators are ineffective at building strong communication.
- When we have noble goals for our motivation, we are more likely to gain respect and achieve success.
- We should do good things for the right reasons, not for credit or attention.
- To ensure that your motives are pure, do extravagant acts of kindness without telling anyone else.

## IMPLEMENTATION

Consider your relationships with others, and honestly reflect upon what factors motivate your conversations and communications with them. If you are driven by negative motivators, attempt to reframe your mindset.

# 1 Consideration

# 2 Motivation

# 3 Appreciation

"Be somebody who makes everybody feel like a somebody."

—*Kid President*

# 4 Validation

# 5 Conversation

# 6 Celebration

# Appreciation

I t had been a long, frustrating day—the kind where you almost expect everything to go wrong. I had been contracted to give a keynote address and training sessions in a small, remote southern town. After working all day on fundraising for my school, the event required me to fly for two hours, rent a car, and drive for another three hours. The airport parking lot had been full, causing me to run through the terminal, only to find that the pelting rain had delayed my flight for two hours. Before I boarded the plane, I made two fatal flaws: I changed into comfortable blue jeans, flip-flops, and a T-shirt, and I checked my suitcase. Normally, I never check my luggage, but I would be gone for several days (it was summer break), and my workshop materials required a larger suitcase than a simple carry-on would accommodate.

After a bumpy flight, during which I endured a gaggle of loud, lively women discussing their scrapbooking techniques, I was, let's say, in a rather foul mood. As I approached the baggage carousel, I stood and watched in dismay as the winding machinery went around and around and, one by one, every suitcase was claimed. Every suitcase but mine. Desperation rose within me. With a transfixed gaze, I attempted to will my bag to magically appear. Tears of frustration stung my eyes. It was one of those moments where I knew that I was being overly dramatic, but exhaustion was defeating my ability to control my emotions. I took a deep breath and headed toward the lost baggage office.

The line was short—only three individuals were ahead of me; however, their rude demeanor and sour expressions were matched by those of the airline employee as she curtly asked each of them a series of questions. The wait seemed interminable, and my anxiety welled up inside of me with each tick of the clock.

My baggage had been lost before, but here was my dilemma: I was exhausted. It was approaching 8:00 p.m., and I still had a three-hour drive ahead. I had no professional clothes to wear for my keynote, and I didn't have my workshop materials. Even if they found my suitcase, how would it get to me when I would be staying at a motor lodge in the middle of nowhere? Would I be required to wait at the airport for several hours before it materialized?

I took a deep breath and did my best to explain my situation to the baggage agent, my voice cracking with frustration. She was highly unimpressed. "It might be on the next flight. I'm not sure, but you are welcome to wait here. It lands at 9:00." And I had been right—no one would deliver my suitcase to my remote location before the following afternoon if it turned up.

*That's it? It **might** be on the next flight? No one knows for sure?* I went into emergency back-up plan mode. While waiting for the 9:00 flight to land, I decided I would go ahead and rent my car, drive to the town's Walmart (the only open store), and attempt to find something suitable to wear in the event that my bag didn't arrive. I would wait until the next flight landed before starting my drive. It sounded like a great plan.

I asked one favor of the baggage reclamation agent: "Can I possibly call you when the next flight lands so that you can tell me if my bag is on it? That way, I will know if I should drive back to the airport, park, and retrieve it." She reluctantly agreed and gave me the direct phone number to the office. I felt immeasurably better. I had a plan, and I would make the best of it.

I wandered aimlessly around Walmart, waiting for the next flight to land. I called at 9:00, but no one answered the phone. Despite my repeated attempts to reach the baggage claim office, the phone kept going to voicemail. I also realized (too late) that the airline agent had not given me any type of baggage-tracking number so that I could call the main 800 number.

I made my purchases at Walmart, and sixty-two dollars later, I drove back to the airport, seething. I planned in detail how I would express my dissatisfaction with this unprofessional, rude woman. One call—that was all I had asked for, and she wouldn't even answer the phone. I quickly parked—illegally—and marched inside. She was nowhere to be found, so I asked the young man at the rental-car desk beside the baggage office if he knew where she was. He explained that she'd been on a break for about thirty minutes.

I sat on a bench and fumed. And waited. In the distance, I finally saw her approaching. Ever so slowly, she trudged toward me, shoulders slumped. Her hair was disheveled and in desperate need of a color retouch. She hugged her slouchy gray sweater around herself as though she wanted to disappear inside of it. I studied her face. It must have been very pretty once, but wrinkled lines formed deep crevasses, etching a permanent frown. It was impossible to know if it had been age or circumstances that had made her look so old.

As this broken woman approached, something in me softened and I felt ashamed. I really saw this woman for the first time. I felt like the Grinch when his heart grew and exploded from his chest. It appeared that this woman was having a much worse day than I was, and for all I knew, every day was the same for her.

I followed her into the baggage office, took a deep breath, and completely changed my approach: "Ma'am, I don't know if you remember me, but I was here a couple of hours ago. I am the one who lost my bag on the delayed flight, and I would like to see if it came in on the next flight." She didn't look at me.

I continued, "You may not realize this, but right now, you are the most important person in my universe. You have the power to completely transform my day, and I would be eternally grateful if you could help me."

She glanced up for the first time, a small smile forming in the corners of her mouth. Her tone changed. "Let me check, sweetie, to see if it made it on that flight."

As she typed in the information, I continued, "You know, it seems like you have a really tough job. You have to spend your day fixing problems that you didn't create. When people come to you, they must usually be frustrated. I apologize if I was one of those people. It must be awful when people take out their anger on you, especially when you weren't the one who lost the bags in the first place!"

She readily agreed and said that people had been jumping on her all day. And then she looked down and said under her breath, "Actually, they jump on me every day."

I added, "Well, I appreciate the work you do. I know that people take it out on you, but thank you for helping people. What you do is significant."

She stood up straight, a radiant smile spreading across her face. The frown lines briefly disappeared, and she looked ten years younger.

"Thank you, sweetheart. I really needed to hear that." Her eyes grew moist. She swallowed hard. "It looks like your suitcase made it. I am going to go and grab it for you."

She was back in a flash. I thanked her profusely, and she smiled and hugged me. The three-hour drive didn't seem so bad after that. I felt an overwhelming sense of peace. I was grateful to have my suitcase, but more importantly, I was grateful to know that I had made someone's day a little bit brighter.

At the beginning of this situation, I had completely failed to follow the first two principles—*consideration* and *motivation*. Initially, I was completely unaware of the baggage agent's perspective, and I was motivated by anger and frustration. **The first two principles are about mindset, and they affect our tone and approach.** They affect the words we choose to say and the sincerity with which we say them. **If you are able to follow these first two principles internally, then the third principle of *appreciation* will be easier to outwardly express.**

I didn't appreciate the baggage agent during my first interaction; I treated her like she was a part of the problem. I didn't say unkind words, but I certainly did not have an appreciative tone. Once I checked myself, I considered the situation from her perspective. And although I was still motivated to get my suitcase, I was also motivated to make this woman's day a little better. It was then that I realized I needed to show her appreciation and let her know that someone was grateful for the job she was doing. Would I have gotten my suitcase either way? Probably. But her night and mine were significantly brightened once I shared sincere words of gratitude.

## THE POWER OF APPRECIATION

*Appreciation* has power—power to transform perspective, power to uplift and inspire, and power to initiate change. Words of appreciation acknowledge and show gratitude:

*Thank you for the work you have done.*

*I appreciate all that you do here.*

*Thank you for sharing your talents with us. You are a huge asset.*

*The work you did was amazing, and I appreciate you.*

> *Appreciation* has power—power to transform perspective, power to uplift and inspire, and power to initiate change.

*I am so very grateful for your help.*

*You always make things better, and I am grateful for that.*

*I want you to know that I notice all the effort you have put into this, and I thank you.*

**Even if someone is sharing grievances with you, appreciate that it is better to know what the other party is thinking and feeling so that you can find a solution.** Wouldn't you rather know where the other person is coming from than for them to be discussing their displeasure with everyone else but you? Here's what it might sound like to show sincere appreciation, even when you don't especially like what has been said:

*Thank you for taking the time to share your concerns with me.*

*I appreciate you setting up this time to talk so that we can find a solution.*

*I am grateful for your time. It means a lot to me.*

*It is helpful to hear what you are feeling. Thank you for telling me.*

*I am grateful that you trust me with your concerns.*

*I appreciate that you have been so open with me about your frustrations.*

Quite often we feel appreciation on the inside, but we fail to communicate it to others. It is important to show appreciation through your actions, but when you look someone directly in the eyes and say, "I am grateful," your words have the power to empower, encourage, heal, and mend. And you will find that when you are intentional about speaking words of appreciation, your awareness of your gratitude increases as well.

## THE CULTURE OF APPRECIATION

When I was the principal (and also still a classroom teacher) at my former school, I was fortunate to teach the Kelly boys—three rambunctious, delightful young men who were full of life. I absolutely adored them. The year that I was going through my divorce, I taught Ian Kelly. His mother, Gaylyn, was the kind of parent I wished I could clone. Throughout the year, I would find random notes from her in my mailbox. The words, often written on sticky notes, contained encouragement, positive quotes, Bible verses, and appreciation. On one particularly rough day, I went to my mailbox to find a small sticky note that simply said, "Thank you for all you do." It soothed my soul in that moment and gave me life—I kept it on my dashboard for weeks. Now I have the blessing of Tatanisha Copeland in my life. She's another mama who sends me encouragement and appreciation through simple text messages: "Checking in! Hope you are having a great day. Team Copeland loves and appreciates you!" Can you imagine how our world would change if we could all be like Mrs. Kelly and Mrs. Copeland? Can you imagine how much more productive your team would be if they felt appreciated in this way?

Whether it's with your boss, coworkers, employees, customers, or your students, spouse, children, or friends—learning to openly express appreciation in a variety of ways will improve your relationships and your ability to communicate effectively. It will especially help when the going gets tough and you need to have a difficult conversation about a disagreement or a misunderstanding.

At the Ron Clark Academy, we believe in the importance of teaching our students to express appreciation often. (After all, to be able to express it outwardly, you must truly take time to internally reflect upon being grateful for the opportunities and blessings that you have been given. This is a wonderful life lesson.) Because gratitude is deeply ingrained in our school culture, it is not uncommon for our teachers to receive thank-you emails from our students, just because. Isn't that beautiful?

**From Ayzia . . .**

*Mrs. Bearden, you are like a second mother to me! Every morning seeing your face and being embraced by your warm hugs permanently remains in my heart. Every day hearing you preach optimism no matter what happens and seeing you smile through adversity makes me want to be a better person. Mrs. Bearden, I honestly don't know where I would be without you telling me in the fifth grade I could write. I don't know where I would be if you didn't sit me down and tell me, "You have something special." I don't know where I would be without you transforming my whole life by giving me the opportunity to get my entire house redone. You brought hope back into me. I would still be living with no optimism that things can get better. I would be complacent without you.*

*We have so many memories I could never forget like all our St. Louis memories, where we were braiding your hair and climbing on EVERYTHING at the City Museum with you and we were dancing and singing at restaurants and just smiling at the fact that even though you don't like dancing, you were dancing for our joy. How can I forget our mass pillow fights across the school or you flipping and transforming the room into so many great things? Or even last year when I stayed and helped you fix the room for the beach and we sang and talked and laughed all night. Even when we were at your house for a slumber party, and when we had that whole fashion show in your basement. I can never even forget those conversations we had in your car about your teenage years and childhood. I loved so much about our trip to South Africa (I'm laughing even thinking about it) when we locked ourselves out of our room, and all you had to say was, "Doofuses!" I appreciate you pouring your time and effort into working with the class and me. I just appreciate you so much!! You are such a beautiful woman that has a smile that lit a fire inside of many and anyone you approach. And you make so many sacrifices for us when you have so much going on and . . . it's just . . . man. I just love you so much, Mrs. Bearden.*

**Or from Jacobi . . .**

*Good evening, Ms. Bearden! I hope you are having a nice night. I wanted to thank you. First, thank you for nurturing my love for writing. Please know that it has also carried on into my high school career. Second, thank you for always encouraging me. Because of your belief in me, I know that anything I want to be possible can be made possible. Third, thank you for every event that you have ever organized for my classmates and me.*

*Ms. Bearden, you will always remain a light that has shone brightly in my life. You have encouraged me and believed in me so much; that is definitely a debt that I can never repay. Thank you for everything; I will never forget the sacrifices that you have made.*

**Or Regan . . .**

*I wanted to say I hope your summer is going as well as mine. I'd like to say thank you for a year I would never forget. You've pulled things out of me that I didn't know existed and I would like to thank you for that because my confidence in myself boosted. I couldn't ask for a better family because one member isn't like the other. Mrs. Bearden, you are like a mother, teacher, and friend in one. I know I can come to you with anything at any time. You warm my heart every time you hug me. Mr. Clark, you gave me that push to put fear aside to go for it and not be afraid. You never gave up on me to reach for the stars. I love you guys and my RCA family! Once again thank you for a great year.*

**Or Amari . . .**

*Dear Mr. Clark and Mrs. Bearden,*

*As I reflect on this past year, I want to thank you for making 2017 so amazing for me! I've grown so much and have learned an immense amount in such a short period. I've seen things and experienced new places all because of you two. There are so many fun moments that I know I will never forget. Thank you for selecting me to be a part of the RCA family. My life has forever changed in the best way because of it! I love you both! Happy New Year and see you in a couple of days!*

Imagine if you could create an organization where it is not uncommon to open your email to find letters like these awaiting you. It would fuel your soul, wouldn't it? Well, you can create such a place. As a leader, it all starts with you.

## LEAD BY EXAMPLE

When you model appreciation, you set the standard. You can help individuals realize how good it feels not only to be uplifted, but also to uplift others.

When it comes to this third principle, it is important to note that as an effective leader, you must allow yourself to receive appreciation, too. When

I was younger and others would pay me a compliment, I would often deflect it. Sometimes it was out of insecurity; other times I thought I was just being humble. I have since learned that there is nothing more annoying than giving thanks to someone, only to have the person refuse to receive it.

> **Someone else:** Kim, your speech was really moving today. Thank you!

> **Me:** Thank you for saying that, but I felt like I veered from my point in the middle, and I talked too fast.

Or . . .

> **Someone else:** Kim, thank you for this picture. I love it!

> **Me:** Well, you look good in it, but my hair is a hot mess. What is that weird thing my bangs are doing?

You get the picture. Annoying. When someone says "thank you" or compliments you, receive it. Say "thank you," smile, and let it wash over you. Then pour your thanks over someone else.

## CHAPTER SUMMARY

- Appreciation should be expressed outwardly and often.

- Appreciation has the power to uplift, transform, and inspire others.

- We must show appreciation even when you disagree with others. Be thankful to be made aware of their thoughts and feelings.

- You are the key to creating a culture of appreciation in your organization.

- You must learn to receive appreciation as freely as you give it.

## IMPLEMENTATION

Use every opportunity to show others your appreciation, and work on finding multiple ways to express your thanks. Even when facing a difficult exchange, begin with a sincere expression of gratitude for the opportunity to find a solution.

1 Consideration

2 Motivation

3 Appreciation

# 4 Validation

"The greatest need of a human being is to be understood, validated and appreciated."

—*Stephen R. Covey*

5 Conversation

6 Celebration

# Validation

When I had the honor of winning the Disney American Teacher Award, I had the privilege of meeting Oprah Winfrey for the very first time. I was definitely star struck, for like countless fans, I had always admired her greatly. The Disney Awards were aired on national television, and the show was a star-studded event held at the Shrine Auditorium in Los Angeles. Disney did everything in a very grand fashion, and they even provided the gowns and tuxedos for the teacher honorees. After the televised portion of the show was over, the teacher honorees and celebrities in attendance gathered on the stage for photos.

I anxiously approached Ms. Winfrey with the hopes of simply shaking her hand. Instead, she turned to me, took both of my hands, looked into my eyes, and told me that my dress was fabulous. She congratulated me and thanked me for being a teacher, and then she proceeded to ask about me—where I taught, what I did, and why I loved teaching. She listened to every word. It was as if the rest of the world had disappeared, and it were only she and I, holding hands like dear friends and sharing a moment.

Ladies and gentlemen, herein lies one of the key secrets to Oprah Winfrey's magic: Ms. Winfrey makes others feel *validated*. When I walked away from that conversation, my first thought wasn't about how great she is; it was about *how important she made me feel*. Ms.

Winfrey is about genuinely, sincerely lifting up the others whom she encounters. Everyday people like me.

Ms. Winfrey didn't act rushed, she didn't look around at others while she was talking to me—she seemed to want to talk to me and learn more about me—Kim, a hardworking teacher. She validated who I am and what I do.

In our day-to-day lives, we encounter countless individuals who either lift us up or let us down. Our bosses, coworkers, neighbors, friends, and family members each leave an indelible impression upon us. But when we feel like we are not only appreciated but also validated, then we are ready to move mountains. Ms. Winfrey used the power of validation to make me feel like being a teacher was every bit as important as her work as a woman who runs an empire.

*Validation* is the principle we use to show that we fully recognize someone's perspective, talents, efforts, feelings, and frustrations. It requires you not only to appreciate others but to go a step further and seek to learn more about them. When you validate others, you look them in the eyes, and you see them. The language of validation often begins with digging deeper and/ or asking questions:

*Tell me more about the background work you have put into this.*

*You did an amazing job. How did you come up with the inspiration to do it?*

*I admire you so much. How do you handle all of this at once?*

*You are always so calm under pressure. Can you give me some of your secrets?*

*I need your expertise. Can I get your input on this?*

*Tell me more about yourself.*

*Talk to me about the process you followed.*

*I can't even begin to imagine how you pulled this off! I want to hear how you did it!*

When talking to children, it is important to validate their positive behaviors that demonstrate respect, honesty, grit, hard work, determination, kindness, and compassion. Teach them that true strength of character is shown through both their words and their actions; for example, instead of just saying, "You are so wonderful!" try to be specific:

> *You really showed tremendous respect to me when you did what I asked.*

> *It took courage for you to be so honest, and I am proud of you.*

> *You have been so strong during this tough time, and I admire that.*

> *You worked so hard on this, and it is okay for you to feel sad about the outcome.*

> *I see how hard you have been working on improving your grades.*

> *I notice how you are always kind to your classmates.*

> *When you shared your ideas with others, you really tried to understand their perspectives.*

Validation should not be confused with hollow praise; do not say something that is not true in an attempt to make someone feel better. Your sincerity matters. If you are disingenuous, others will not take anything you say to heart. Forced compliments or feigned interest in someone do not benefit anyone; in fact, they can be misleading and cause confusion or harm to your organization.

> Your sincerity matters. If you are disingenuous, others will not take anything you say to heart.

## IF YOU DON'T HAVE ANYTHING NICE TO SAY . . .

What do you do if you are about to have a conversation with someone who is, well, a hot mess? What if you don't have any complimentary words to say? Validation is still necessary. You can validate the person's feelings instead—acknowledge their situation, stressors, or obstacles.

When people feel heard, they are more receptive to suggestions for improvement.

> *This was a huge task to accomplish. What made it the most difficult for you?*
>
> *If it were a perfect world, what would you have changed about this situation?*
>
> *Are you having a tough day? It seems that you have so much on you right now. How can I help make it better for you?*
>
> *It can be difficult to be new, here. How are you feeling right now? What things are going well for you? What keeps you up at night?*
>
> *On a scale of one to ten, how stressed are you right now? How can we get that to a more reasonable number?*
>
> *Talk to me about your frustrations.*

In digging deeper and validating others, you are actually helping the person self-reflect. You can help others recognize their successes, and they will be better able to realize and articulate areas for their own needed improvement.

A word of caution: When validating others, be careful not to use condescending language. You should not tell others that you know how they feel; you should ask how they feel.

> **Condescending language:** I know exactly how it feels to be in your position, and I know that it is difficult to go on with enthusiasm.
>
> **Validating language:** When I found myself in a similar situation, I found it hard to stay optimistic. Is that how you are feeling?

In your attempts to validate another, you should not say that you know exactly what it is like to be in that person's situation. It can be offensive and seem as though you are minimizing someone's experience without even knowing what his or her journey has been. Empathize, but acknowledge that you cannot truly know what it is to walk in another's shoes. Listen more than you speak to seek to understand. This will be what truly validates the other person.

# THE VORTEX OF NEGATIVITY

Ron Clark once pointed out a fascinating phenomenon to me: Listen to a conversation where someone is sharing a concern or frustration, and watch how others will try to one-up the person with a more fantastical story. It might go something like this conversation among three coworkers:

**Mildred:** I am sorry I am late! I am having a horrible morning! My refrigerator stopped working, and I had to scramble to put most of the food in coolers.

**Madge:** Girl, I feel you! My day has been awful, too! I got a ticket coming into work because my tag expired, and I haven't had the time to get it updated. It is going to cost me even more money than your refrigerator!

**Veronica:** Well, both of y'all might be having a hard day, but my transmission is about to go out. And when my refrigerator went out, it leaked all over my kitchen floor.

Do you see what happened here? In an attempt to validate and show Mildred that they knew how she felt, Madge and Veronica shared their own drama. This doesn't validate Mildred at all; instead, it minimizes her feelings by implying that *well, at least your situation isn't as bad as mine.* This kind of commiserating also leads conversations into a vortex of negativity.

Now imagine if the conversation had gone this way instead:

**Mildred:** I am sorry I am late! I am having a horrible morning! My refrigerator stopped working, and I had to scramble to put most of the food in coolers.

**Madge:** Oh, my gosh. I am sorry! I hope a lot of food wasn't ruined! What can I do to help you get ready for the day? Do you need anything? Would you like me to watch your class for a few minutes while you catch your breath?

**Veronica:** Oh, Mildred! How frustrating! Let me go make your copies for you. And when you are ready, I know a great repairman that I used when my refrigerator stopped working. Would you like me to get his information for you?

**Mildred:** Thank you both for being so understanding. I am so grateful for your help!

In the second scenario, Mildred feels heard. Her feelings are validated, and her coworkers are led to offer help and solutions. They make the conversation about Mildred, not themselves, and in this situation, that is how it should be.

## SEEING WHAT GOES UNNOTICED

Validation is all about creating moments for others; it is a language of support. If you change your language to validate others, you will find that you will be led to do more for others. Why? Because you are in a mindset where you hear and see them, and things are no longer just about you.

As a teacher and an administrator, I have the opportunity to interact with some amazing mamas—mamas who pour their hearts and souls into everything for their children. They are women who sacrifice without hesitation and give without expectations. And sometimes they get bone tired, and yes, like all of us, they can have moments of hysteria.

> Validation is all about creating moments for others; it is a language of support.

A couple of years ago, I was accosted in the parking lot by such a mama. She ranted, "Mrs. Bearden, I am done! Just done! I cannot do this anymore!"

"Oh, Ms. Flynn, let me help. Let's go inside," I said, gently taking her arm to guide her out of view of the other parents waiting to pick up their children. A crying mama in the parking lot is never a good thing, but more importantly, I could tell that she truly was at a breaking point.

We went inside and sat down in an empty classroom. I said, "Talk to me. Let it all out. I am listening."

Ms. Flynn had lost her cool when her daughter handed her a detention for a missing assignment, and when she had said she was done, she had meant with her daughter, not us. She was angry at her daughter for not doing all that she was supposed to do even though this mama was working two jobs and doing all that she could to provide for them. To add to her challenges, she was caring for a sick brother and watching his kids, too, in a home that was not nearly large enough on a salary that was not large enough to make ends meet.

After thanking her for opening up to me, I said, "Ms. Flynn, you are doing a wonderful job of taking care of everybody, but is there anyone taking care of you?"

And the tears flowed harder. I just sat and hugged her while I rubbed her back and said, "Let it all out."

When she eventually spoke, she said that she was all alone with no help. She told me she had not done a single thing for herself in two years. It had been two years since she had left the house to do anything other than go to work, attend a school event, or care for her family members.

"Ms. Flynn," I said, "I want you to know that I see you. I see what a wonderful mother you are. Your daughter is a wonderful child, too. Even good kids make mistakes sometimes. Your influence upon her is obvious—she is truly a phenomenal little girl. I wish I could give you a night on the town where you could just relax and let someone take care of you!"

She shared how it felt good just to have someone listen to her. She said she didn't expect me to fix anything; she just needed to talk to someone and vent.

When she left, I thought about all of the mamas of my students. On any given day, any number of them probably feel unseen and underappreciated. I decided then and there that I would have a night for them—a night to do nothing but validate them. RCA Ladies' Night was born.

I went home and crafted an invitation for my mamas, aunts, and grandmamas to attend an evening that was just for them. For the attire, I told them that they could wear anything from pajamas to cocktail—whatever made them feel fabulous. I secured volunteers to serve them and sponsors to cover the cost.

I spent the next few weeks preparing for the big night, and the buzz was huge. The mamas were all RSVPing. They secured sitters and marked their calendars for our Saturday night together.

And then my own mama took a turn for the worse. My mama had been suffering from Alzheimer's for three years, but during the weeks leading up to the event, we discovered she was also in the last stages of cancer. The end was near, and she was moved into a hospice facility where she could be treated with round-the-clock, tender loving care. I stayed by her side for the week she was there, crawling into bed with her to hold her at night. She was unconscious, but the doctors said that hearing is always the last thing to go. So I held her and stroked her hair, and as tears streamed down my face, I poured words of appreciation and validation into my own mama. She passed quietly and peacefully on Friday night, surrounded by her family who loved her so. It was the evening before RCA Ladies' Night was supposed to take place.

Emails poured in, expressing love and condolences. Everyone assumed I would cancel the event, but my mama had always loved a party, and I couldn't think of a better way to honor her than to continue with my plan.

The next day, a team of wonderful volunteers arrived to help me set up. The tables were lined with candles, and the food was beautifully arranged. As each mama arrived, I hugged her tightly. A photographer was there to capture each arrival, and the women were overjoyed. And then in walked one of our mamas in full cocktail attire—shimmering from her dangling earrings to her bejeweled shoes. She was a showstopper, a true vision of beauty. We had never seen her like this, and every woman stood and applauded when she entered. She was moved to tears. You see, she told me that she, too, had wanted to dress up for so long but had not had anywhere to go.

> They were all wonderful mothers, but they each have an identity of their own that should be celebrated.

We enjoyed dinner together, and the sweet volunteers served the mamas and took care of their every need. I set ground rules for the evening: There could be no conversations about their children. I explained that they were all wonderful mothers, but they each have an identity of their own that should be celebrated. I placed a variety of questions on the table to start conversations:

*What did you dream of doing when you were a little girl?*

*What were you like in high school?*

*If you had one talent you do not possess, what would it be?*

*What would we be surprised to know about you?*

After dinner, two of our mothers with voices like angels sang, and then I shared my story and words of encouragement. As I hugged each of them goodbye, the women thanked me repeatedly for validating them and making them feel special. I knew my own mama had been right there with me all along, pleased beyond measure.

And now, RCA Ladies' Night is a yearly tradition, designed to validate women for the influence they have. For me personally, it is to pay homage to my own mama while reminding me of the importance of appreciating and validating those who gave us all life. What could be better than that?

## CHAPTER SUMMARY

- Validation is the language we use to show that we fully recognize another's perspective, talents, efforts, feelings, and frustrations.

- Validation requires you to dig deeper and ask questions to learn more about the other party.

- When showing validation, be careful not to be condescending.

- When validating children, focus on acknowledging their positive behaviors.

- When you are struggling to validate someone's attributes, validate feelings instead.

- When you validate others, you will feel validated, too.

## IMPLEMENTATION

When communicating with others, ask questions about their actions and feelings so that you can validate them. Acknowledge the importance of their stories.

# 1 Consideration

# 2 Motivation

# 3 Appreciation

# 4 Validation

# 5  Conversation

"Tone is often the most important part of a conversation—and listening is so much more important than what you say."

—*Hoda Kotb*

# 6 Celebration

# Conversation

The hotel ballroom was beautifully decorated. Ambient lighting cast rose-colored shadows across the crisp white linens on the candlelit tables. Magnificent floral centerpieces graced tables set with fine china and crystal, and the harpist's melodies lilted overhead. It was obvious that the corporation had spared no expense to make this awards night a special one.

As the guest keynote speaker for the event, I sat at one of the head tables, joined by two of the company's chief officers and other colleagues from their department who were being recognized for their hard work. And although I am comfortable engaging in conversation with new acquaintances, I couldn't get a word in edgewise. None of us could. You see, one of the company's leaders—I will call him Bill—completely monopolized the conversation. Bill talked about his hard work, his exhaustion, and his own accomplishments. He then moved on to his golf game, his favorite sports teams, and the problems with his new Lexus. And his Rolex wasn't keeping good time. *Can you imagine the stress of that?* From there, the conversation turned to the amazing accomplishments of his uber-successful, attractive children. He was loud, pompous, and completely obnoxious.

I am an observer of people, and time and time again, I watched his employees roll their eyes at one another when he would look in the opposite direction. A couple of times, they even had to suppress laughter at the ridiculousness of it all. Whenever one of them would try to interject a remark, he would quickly speak over them and continue on with his lengthy discourse. The woman beside me even leaned over and whispered into my ear, "We apologize for him. It is always all about him. I am sorry." This was supposed to be *their* night, yet they felt dismissed, disregarded, and disrespected. In an attempt to impress them with his weighty résumé, Bill had completely hijacked the table and the moods of everyone.

Do you know a Bill? Most of us do. Somewhere along the way, Bill got the false idea that during a conversation, he should do all the talking. Bill might have thought that he would gain respect by relaying his résumé and telling everyone how fabulous his life was, but all that talking had just the opposite effect. It is safe to say that Bill didn't take into consideration the perspective of others and was motivated by selfish ambition and ego (or perhaps insecurity). And as far as appreciation goes, well, he only showed appreciation for himself and his children. Bill never thanked the awardees for their hard work, and he certainly never validated them.

*Conversation* involves an exchange of thoughts, ideas, and feelings. It is about listening as much as it is about speaking. When you have meaningful conversation, you engage in a constant stream of *participation, hesitation, information*, and *clarification*. These factors do not have to be done sequentially; rather, there is a continuous ebb and flow to each of them depending on the circumstances.

> When you have meaningful conversation, you engage in a constant stream of participation, hesitation, information, and clarification.

## PARTICIPATION

Participation draws others into the dialogue; you ensure that everyone is a part of the discussion. Are you monopolizing what is being said, or is there an even exchange? Here's what participation sounds like:

*Rajeev, what is your take on this? Do you agree?*

*Jerome, are you also taking a vacation this summer? Where are you planning to go?*

*Natasha, do you have anything to add?*

*Stephen, I haven't heard from you. What is your opinion?*

*Maya, this reminds me of the story you shared with me the other day. You have got to tell everyone what happened!* (Note: If you are tempted to tell Maya's story for her when she is sitting right there, then you are probably being a Bill. Give her the moment to shine!)

## HESITATION

Do you take time to pause to let others interject their ideas? Do you pause to reflect upon their meaningful comments before responding? If you are busy thinking about what you want to say while another person is still talking, you are not truly focusing upon what they are saying. Do you cut others off or give them the chance to formulate their points? In the world of education, we call this "wait time." When asking students questions, many teachers grow uncomfortable with silence, and they tend to answer their own questions or to call upon the smartest kid when the best response might just be a few moments away. To make sure people listen when others talk at RCA, we do not allow students to raise their hands while someone else is speaking. They must wait until the speaker is finished so that they will truly listen to what is being said. Learn to be comfortable with silence; it can speak as loudly as words.

> Learn to be comfortable with silence; it can speak as loudly as words.

# INFORMATION

When providing information, it is important to be accurate and honest. Do you provide detailed facts when necessary? Are you able to do so clearly and concisely? Do you offer meaningful content that provides support, offers suggestions, solves a problem, or informs the listener?

*I understand your point. May I offer a few things to consider?*

*Let me tell you what I have learned.*

*Here are the details that I do know . . .*

*I looked into this before we met, and I have some answers to your questions.*

*Based on what I have experienced, I have some ideas for ways to help.*

*Here is what happened . . .*

*This is what I saw . . .*

You should also use consideration and tact when sharing difficult truths. I was chatting with a principal who told me that one of her teachers completely offended a mother at a parent conference when she said, "I am not sure if your child is just slow or lazy, but he isn't performing well enough to pass my class."

Ouch. Statements like this can leave the parent feeling hurt and upset or angry and defensive. If your motivation is to help the child and to help the parent, you have to express accurate information in a way that can be received. Perhaps the teacher could have said, "I am concerned about your child. I am still trying to determine what factors are behind his lack of success. I am not sure if the material is too difficult for him or if he is not putting forth his best effort. Do you have any insight that you can share?"

Can you see how the second statement could lead to a far more productive outcome? When providing information, always consider the connotations behind the words you use and the way that you use them. Let's try some other examples:

**Unproductive comment:** Your daughter is loose, and all of the boys are talking about her posts on social media.

**Productive comment:** I am concerned about the way your daughter is being perceived by some of the other students. It is possible that she is projecting an image that is unbecoming to her reputation, and I really want to help. Have you seen her social media posts?

**Unproductive comment:** Your son is never going to pass and get into a good school, because he doesn't care enough.

**Productive comment:** I am here for your son, but when I have met with him to discuss his current situation, he seems apathetic. Am I misinterpreting his emotions? Do you think that he has shut down because he is overwhelmed or because something else is happening? How can I help? I really want to see him succeed, and I don't want his current efforts to keep him from getting into a good school.

## CLARIFICATION

Notice that in the comments above, I also asked for more insight to make sure that my information was correct. I sought out *clarification*, which is another factor of effective conversation. Here's what it might sound like to ask additional or deeper questions that show you are interested and you care:

*I think you might have a great solution for our problem. Would you tell us your idea one more time?*

*Can you explain your vision for the project to everyone here so that we can ask any questions we might have?*

*Your father is sick? I am so sorry. How can I help you?*

*You love to travel? Where is your favorite place to visit?*

When you seek clarification, be mindful not to be nosy. Be careful not to probe into people's private matters unless they freely share a confidential topic with you.

**Clarifying statement:** Tell me about your family.

**Nosy:** You don't have kids? Why not? When do you think you will have them?

Additionally, if someone shares a struggle with you, you must remember to follow up to show that you really cared about the questions you asked. Let's pretend, for example, that your coworker opens up to share that she is concerned about her father who is having back surgery the following week. You care—you really do—but then life gets in the way, and you forget about it. You must find a way to remember to circle back with your coworker. If you have too many things filling your mind (like most of us do), then simply set a calendar reminder for yourself. On the night before the surgery, send a quick text or email that says, "Thinking about your father and you. I hope it all goes well tomorrow! Let me know if you need anything!" Or on the day after the surgery, call and say, "I just wanted to make sure your dad is doing well and to let you know I am here for you." Maybe another coworker tells you something exciting, like that his daughter is competing in a national gymnastics competition. The same applies. Send words of encouragement or congratulations. Do you see how this validates someone else? If you forget to say anything, your coworker might end up feeling worse than if you had never had a meaningful conversation in the first place.

> If someone shares a struggle with you, you must remember to follow up to show that you really cared about the questions you asked.

## LEARNING THE ART OF CONVERSATION

At the Ron Clark Academy, we teach our students the art of conversation. We role play discussions, and we show them how to ask probing questions and dig deeper. Many of our students are introverts by nature, and introversion is a beautiful personality type. Contrary to what many think, introverts do like people; they just need time alone to refuel and recharge. When it comes to discussions, your introverts often have the best ideas because they don't just blurt out whatever comes to mind. They first digest what's been said and reflect upon their thoughts before sharing them. So how do you get introverts to engage in the conversation? Participation, hesitation, information, and clarification.

We also have one more trick: Each summer, our staff writes the name of every child on a separate piece of paper, and we spread the papers around a large room. We give every adult in our school round sticker dots—red, yellow, and blue. A red dot means that you feel like you have birthed that child: You know the child's hobbies, interests, hopes, and dreams. You feel like this is a child with whom you will stay in contact forever. A blue dot is for students whom you know well and with whom you feel a close bond. A yellow dot means that you have a nice rapport with the child, but beyond that, the relationship is limited. We only give our staff members a certain number of dots because in reality, we all only have a certain amount of time and energy. We put on some relaxing music, and our staff goes around the room and places the dots.

Afterward, we pull the sheets together and categorize them, taking special note of the students with the fewest dots or no dots at all. These are students who could be in danger of slipping through the cracks because our staff is not as connected to them. We want to know every child, and we want all children to know that they have a voice that needs to be heard; therefore, we commit to engaging on a deeper level with the students whom we do not know as well. So what does this look like? At lunchtime, even though you might want to sit with the kid with the red dots because he is so fun, you go sit with the kid with no dots and get to know him. Look, I could eat lunch with Jericho every day. He and I just click, and he is so very adorable! But I often go sit by a no-dot kid. Inevitably, Jericho comes

> We want to know every child, and we want all children to know that they have a voice that needs to be heard.

and joins our discussion (we are tight like that), but I am focusing on building new relationships at the same time. When I see students at school events or in the hallways, I seek out the students with whom I need to build a rapport to ask them about their day or their plans for the weekend.

We will also pull together these students and have a conversation. (By the way, we certainly do not tell them that they have the "no-dot" distinction.) We give these students something meaningful to talk about, such as spirit day ideas, ways to improve lunch, or some other kid-related issue. When you put all of those kids in one room without the more outspoken and extroverted students, a fascinating phenomenon occurs: They become more vocal. They share amazing ideas. They shine.

Now, if you are working in a major organization full of adults, the dot activity might not be practical. But what if you had that mindset? What if you worked harder to develop a rapport with those who are harder to get to know? What if you sought them out for ideas or advice? In doing so, they would feel appreciated and validated; additionally, they might have the very best ideas of all to add to your organization. They might even have the solution that you have desperately been seeking all along.

# CHAPTER SUMMARY

- Conversation involves an exchange of thoughts, ideas, information, and feelings.

- When conversing with others, we should listen as much as we speak.

- Meaningful conversation has a constant stream of participation, hesitation, information, and clarification.

- When we seek to develop a rapport with others, we are able to learn more about their insights and solutions.

# IMPLEMENTATION

Be mindful of how much you speak during conversations with others. If you find that you are monopolizing the conversation, take a deep breath and stop talking. Ask the other people in the room for their thoughts, ideas, and input. Remember that a conversation is an exchange, not a soliloquy.

1 Consideration

2 Motivation

3 Appreciation

4 Validation

5 Conversation

# 6  Celebration

"The more you praise and celebrate your life, the more there is in life to celebrate."

—Oprah Winfrey

# Celebration

Soweto is a city located near Johannesburg, South Africa. Each year, we at the Ron Clark Academy take our eighth-grade students there to work in schools and orphanages. The beautiful people from Soweto have a rich but very painful history. Soweto was once known as the "Southwest Townships"—a region where people of color were forced to live during apartheid. People of color were categorized as Black or Colored (people thought to be of mixed race) and separated accordingly. Although the word *township* sounds quite lovely, these were not lovely places. Horrible conditions and disparities prevailed, and although apartheid ended in 1994 (just 1994!), the aftereffects of the oppression remain. These inequities are extremely apparent in the schools of Soweto that lack adequate desks, textbooks, and resources. The schools do not have working technology. Some classes sit for hours and wait for instructors to arrive. But when we go to visit, we are always overwhelmed by the beauty of South Africa and the loving spirit of the people; we are captivated by their resilience and their joy.

My trips to South Africa have had a transformative effect on my life. So much so that in June of 2014, three magnificent twelve-year-old Sowetan boys joined our family, and they simultaneously began the seventh grade as students at the Ron Clark Academy. It is a beautiful story filled with incomprehensible love, yet there have been many challenges along the way.

My son Phakamani was born in the Eastern Cape. When his young mother was unable to care for him, he was sent to live with his grandparents who were traveling missionaries. Realizing the need for him to attend school, his grandparents then sent him to live with his cousin, Sisipho (one of my other sons), in Soweto. Sisipho and Phakamani were living in a garage when I met them. Sisipho's biological parents are loving, caring people, but life was very difficult, and they loved their son and nephew so much that they relinquished their parental rights, and I later adopted them (along with my son Sabelo who attended school with them).

All three of my sons have their unique talents and personalities; however, when Phakamani arrived, we had challenges with him. Phakamani is brilliant, charismatic, and athletic. He has a contagious giggle, and a smile that melts the heart. I loved him instantly. Phakamani had never really been parented the way we parent, and he would shut down, even when he was corrected in the smallest of ways. One moment he would be full of joy and laughter; the next moment he would refuse to speak, often hiding under his bed. At times, I viewed it as insubordination. I felt like he was unappreciative and lacked respect.

But I was wrong.

After months of seeking to understand Phakamani while trying to help him, we still had many emotional days where we struggled and conflict prevailed, despite our efforts. My husband Scotty and I continued to show our appreciation for him, and I would validate him and his gifts; however, discipline is necessary when raising a child, and Phakamani would still shut down when we tried to correct him in any way. The constant friction began to consume our household. On one of my most frustrating days, I called my grown daughter Madison, sobbing. I shared my heartbreak with her. She listened, validated our efforts, and simply said, "Mim, (her name for me), you are going to have to love him through it. When you first married Scotty, I could be awful, too. I was afraid to trust him with my heart." And so, my wise daughter encouraged me to stay the course.

A few weeks later, I told Phakamani "no" when he wanted a "yes." He turned around, walked outside, and lay in the grass, staring at the clouds. After a few moments, I walked outside and lay beside him in silence. Finally, I said, "Sweetie, I love you. I chose you—I adopted you because I love you so very much. You fill my heart with so much joy. But when you get like this, I am at a loss. I don't know what else to do. Help me understand. One minute you are so loving, and then next you are so distant. Please talk to me."

After an interminable silence, he finally whispered, "When I get too close to someone, they always send me away."

And there was the answer I had sought for months. Madison had been right—he was afraid to trust us with his heart. "Oh, sweetie, this is your forever home now. You will always be my son. I am not going anywhere, and I am never going to send you away." I reached over and grabbed his hand, tears streaming down my face and onto the grass. It seemed like we lay there for hours, hand in hand, an understanding finally reached. It was a celebration of love, of truth, of acceptance.

Today, Phakamani is my miracle. He has grown into a strong, joyful, caring young man who openly shares his feelings, hopes, and dreams. He is an extremely respectful and appreciative son who consistently radiates enthusiasm, appreciation, affection, love, and joy. His transformation has been life changing for us all. I used all of the six principles with Phakamani over and over, but it still took time. In his case, the wounds were so deep that they could not possibly be healed in one conversation.

Celebration is the way that we express our delight for the opportunity to engage with someone or for our success at reaching an understanding. It can be a handshake or a hug, a smile

> *Celebration* is the way that we express our delight for the opportunity to engage with someone or for our success at reaching an understanding.

or a note of thanks. It can be flowers and champagne, or it can even be sitting in silence, holding hands while watching the clouds. Just like a great book has a phenomenal ending, a great conversation should end with a sense of, "I'm so glad we had this time together."

Ann Cramer is somewhat of a legend in Atlanta. A phenomenal businesswoman, a dedicated philanthropist, and an experienced advisor on every issue imaginable, Ann is asked to be on every committee and every board. She is a tiny woman, but a powerful force to be reckoned with. People love her because she radiates joy and goodwill; she is a true servant leader. We are blessed to have her on the RCA advisory council, and recently, Ron, Kirk Brown (our senior development director), and I met with her to seek advice about our capital campaign for our performing arts center. Ann and her colleague Ann Curry (another phenomenal woman) met with us, giving us sound insight, suggestions, and encouragement. It was a great conversation, and we ended with a celebration of hugs and well wishes.

Before I even reached home, this email was in my inbox:

*Oh, WOW, Dear Ron, Kim, and Kirk—*

*Ann and I were just grinning from ear to ear after our meeting with you three! WOW! Let me say it again! WOW! We were deeply moved by and impressed with your thoughtfulness, preparation, and organization! But even more, we were inspired by your energy, enthusiasm, intellect, and innovative ideas! MANY, many thanks for giving us the opportunity to share in your planning process, and please know that we are always available to meet with you! Best and blessings to you as you launch your trajectory for the next ten years! We are so very proud of YOU! Many, many thanks!*

In case you missed it, Ann thanked us for having the opportunity to give us advice. Can you believe that? We were honored to just be in the room with her and have her ear, and yet she sent this email to us. Notice how she showed appreciation and validated us. This email felt like she sent a birthday party to my inbox. Don't you wish you also had an Ann to go to for advice?

I aspire to be an Ann with my leadership communication. We all should.

It is an honor to have the opportunity to interact with others—a privilege. Always take a final moment to acknowledge the importance of your time together before moving on to something else. After all, life is made from moments, and moments should be celebrated.

## CHAPTER SUMMARY

- Celebration is the way that we express our delight for the opportunity to engage with someone and find success at reaching an understanding.

- A celebration can be simple—a handshake, a hug, or a quick note of acknowledgement.

- By celebrating our time with others, we acknowledge that it is a privilege to be able to connect with them, and we strengthen the relationship.

## IMPLEMENTATION

Find ways to celebrate your time spent with someone else. A hug, a kind gesture, a text message, a note—do something to acknowledge that you are grateful for the exchange you had with one another.

# THE 6 PRINCIPLES

## Internal Dialogue

### 1. Consideration
*What could be the other person's perspective?*

*Thoughts sound like...*

I wonder what could have triggered that email?

Something is obviously going on that I don't understand.

Is she going through some type of personal crisis?

Could we have done something else that upset her, and she is just responding to suppressed anger about it now?

If he is experiencing some type of problems, how can I let him know that we care?

I need to figure out how to fix this for the sake of everyone involved.

### 2. Motivation
*What do I want to be the outcome?*
*What should be driving me?*

| Positive Motivators | | Versus | Negative Motivators | |
|---|---|---|---|---|
| Compassion | Love | | Anger | Ignorance |
| Dedication | Patience | | Attention | Insecurity |
| Determination | Peace | | Control | Jealousy |
| Diligence | Persistence | | Defensiveness | Manipulation |
| Empathy | Positivity | | Ego | Negativity |
| Engagement | Productivity | | Fear | Power |
| Gentleness | Resolution | | Frustration | Revenge |
| Goodness | Service | | Greed | Selfishness |
| Grit | Significance | | Guilt | Sloth |
| Insight | Solutions | | Hatred | Suspicion |
| Joy | Truth | | | |
| Kindness | Wisdom | | | |

## External Dialogue

### 3. Appreciation
*What am I grateful for in this situation?*

*Sounds like...*

Thank you for taking the time to share your concerns with me...

I appreciate you setting up this time to talk so that we can find a solution...

I am grateful for your time. It means a lot to me...

It is helpful to hear what you are feeling. Thank you for telling me...

I am grateful that you trust me with your concerns...

I appreciate that you have been so open with me about your frustrations...

### 4. Validation
*How can I make the other person feel respected and heard?*

*Sounds like...*

I hope you are having a relaxing summer– you deserve it!

You did an amazing job. How did you come up with the inspiration to do it?

How do you handle all of this at once?

This was a huge task to accomplish. What made it the most difficult for you?

If it were a perfect world, what would you have changed about this situation?

Are you having a tough day? How can I help make it better for you?

### 5. Conversation
*What needs to be said and heard?*

**Participation:** What is your take on this? Do you agree? Do you have anything to add?

**Hesitation:** Pause. Listen. Reflect.

**Information:** Let me tell you what I have learned... Here are the details that I do know...

**Clarification:** What do you know about this situation? I think you might have a great solution. Would you tell us your idea one more time?
Can you explain your vision for the project?

### 6. Celebration
*How can we express our success at reaching understanding?*

Examples:

A handshake

A hug

An email

A thank-you note

A text

A follow-up phone call

# Part 2
# Applications and Complications

Now that you have learned the six principles, it is important to think of them as a way of life, not as an isolated set of behaviors. They do not have to be done in a linear fashion, and you do not have to use every principle in every single interaction; however, *consideration* and *motivation* should always be a part of your internal dialogue and mindset if you hope to see a true transformation in your ability to communicate with others more effectively. If you consistently express *appreciation*, provide *validation*, and engage in more meaningful *conversations*, others will notice a change in you. You will find that others will treat you with increased respect—because you have given the gift of respect to them. And that is definitely a cause for *celebration*!

Even with our best attempts at effective communication, life is full of complications; therefore, it is important to develop an awareness of additional factors that can create obstacles to your success. The chapters that follow focus on ways to further refine your skills by preparing you to deal with some of the most common scenarios and challenges that can make communication difficult.

# Preparation

As the grand doors swung open, I watched Ella take a deep breath, smile, and head toward station number one. Eager for the competition to begin, the other students fell in line after her, dutifully streaming toward their own assigned stations. Perfectly polished from head to toe, they carried themselves with poise and professionalism, ready for the challenges, simulations, and surprises that awaited them.

At one station, Naima was interviewed by a local reporter as television cameras recorded her commentary. Close by, Makayla was asked to make a toast to a wedding party, complete with a bride and groom in full wedding apparel. Donovan read a commercial from a teleprompter. Destin received the assignment to fire an employee. Students answered interview questions, engaged in debates, and made speeches, all as a part of RCA's annual Amazing Shake Competition.

Designed to prepare our students for real-world scenarios, the Amazing Shake is Ron's brainchild, and it is one of our students' favorite days of the year. At our school, the students learn soft skills, such as how to give a firm handshake and engage in meaningful conversation. On the day of the Shake, business leaders volunteer to present the challenges and critique our students. Students face thirty different scenarios, and at each, the judges score students on their ability to handle the tasks with confidence, poise, and intellect. After the morning rounds, the top twenty-eight students are whisked away to businesses all over the city, where the challenges intensify. The students have participated in interviews led by corporate executives. They have engaged in debates, discussed current events, and delivered speeches. They have given sales pitches, conducted tours, managed restaurants, and filmed newscasts. The top five students earn a trip to New York City for a day to continue challenges and compete for the top spot. Each year, the Amazing Shake Winner is lauded at our school with great fanfare. So many schools have replicated the event that we now host the Amazing Shake National Competition at the Ron Clark Academy, and students from across the country come to participate.

Why do we go to such great lengths to allow students to practice vital communication skills? Because one of the biggest influencers of success is *preparation*. I want my students to be so prepared that no one will ever have an excuse for not hiring them. I want them to be set apart as global leaders. I want them to feel like they can dine with kings and queens and know how to engage in dialogue with top executives. If you prepare children, you give them a beautiful gift: You empower them for any challenges that life throws their way.

## PREPARATION LEADS TO SUCCESS

As adults, preparation is one of the keys to our success, too. Preparation shows respect, and when you adequately prepare for a meeting, you demonstrate that you value the other person. I have interviewed countless educators over the years, and you might be amazed how many have come to the interview ill prepared. (Actually, if you are an administrator, you might not be surprised at all.)

I had been interviewing candidates for a support position all day long, and although I had seen many strong contenders, I had been looking forward to my next interview the most. She had been recommended by an acquaintance, and I was eager to learn more about her.

I had communicated with her via email, and we had agreed on the 3:00 p.m. time slot; my last candidate for the day would follow at 3:30.

By 3:07, she still had not appeared, nor had she called. Atlanta traffic can be a beast, so I took this into consideration. At 3:13, I watched her walk slowly into the lobby without a care in the world. I thought perhaps I had scheduled her incorrectly, but when she checked in at the desk, she told our office manager, Mrs. Burns, that she was here for her 3:00 p.m. appointment. I introduced myself and led her upstairs to my classroom, and the interview began.

"Ms. Jacobs, it is a pleasure to meet you. I have heard wonderful things about you," I said.

"Thank you," she said. "Can you tell me again who you are?"

"I am Kim Bearden."

"And what is your role here?" she asked.

"I am the cofounder and executive director. I am also the one who communicated with you via email," I said.

"Oh, okay," she replied.

Now, I certainly do not think that everyone should know who on earth I am. But if you have a job interview, go to the organization's website and do your homework. The fact that she didn't know who I was (and I had set up the interview) let me know that she did not adequately prepare. As I peppered her with questions, it became incredibly obvious that she didn't know a thing about our school or what we did, either. It was a waste of both of our time. In contrast, my 3:30 p.m. candidate was on time, and she came with her printed résumé and several other documents. She shared what she knew about us and had even prepared questions that she could not find answers to online. Her preparation impressed me because I believed she would give the same attention to detail to her position. I was right. That candidate, Ms. Williams, got the job, and has been an extraordinary member of our team ever since.

Sometimes circumstances beyond our control force us to be late, but my daddy always taught me that if you are chronically late, you are really saying, "My time is more valuable than yours." If you have an issue with tardiness, add a fifteen-minute buffer to all of your meetings. Set calendar reminders to keep yourself on track. And if you are going to be late, always call and remember to apologize.

> If you are chronically late, you are really saying, "My time is more valuable than yours."

## PREPARATION SHOWS YOU CARE

Preparation can also be a beautiful way to validate others and to express appreciation. Each summer, my staff and I visit the homes of every newcomer to our school. Our purpose is to get to know our students and their families better and to pledge our commitment to working together as a team. In groups of four to five staff members, we visit as many as fifteen homes in a single day, and the process always fills our hearts with joy.

Jaycob was a new student to our school, but he was not new to the RCA family. His older brother Jaydon was one of our beloved alumni, and so we had watched Jaycob grow up long before he was enrolled in our fifth grade. We looked forward to his home visit, mostly because we already felt completely bonded with his family, and we knew that it would be a warm and wonderful exchange. We knew that Jaycob was excited to be a student at RCA, but we had no idea that he was prepared to show us just how excited. As we pulled into the driveway, Mr. Thompson exclaimed, "Look at the banner!"

Jaycob had hand painted an enormous banner that read *TEAM 2020: #RCAROCKS!* And that was just the beginning. As we entered, Jaycob welcomed us to the "RCA Faculty Olympics." He had different colored T-shirts prepared for us. He had even rounded up extra sneakers in case any of us were not dressed to run.

"You already know that my brother Jaydon is really musical, but I wanted you to know that I am really athletic. I like to play outside and make obstacle courses, so I thought we would do one together," he shared, beaming from ear to ear.

It was August. We were hot. We were tired. But Jaycob is one of the most endearing kids on the planet, and so as soon as he extended the invitation, we couldn't wait to get started. He escorted us outside and amazed us with his creativity. He had taken random items—everything from garbage-can lids to boxes to clothesline—and had made an extraordinary obstacle course. As we raced against one another to have the fastest time, Mrs. Barnes, Mrs. Thompson, Mr. Thompson, and I were so tickled that we could hardly walk, much less run. When we collapsed onto the ground, there was Jaycob with fresh hand towels and water bottles. And not just any water bottles; he had made new labels on them that said, "Thank you for letting me be a part of RCA."

The preparation that Jaycob put into that day beautifully demonstrated his appreciation and his respect for the opportunity to be our student. And since that day, he has continued to demonstrate that gratitude. Wouldn't you rather hire someone who joyfully prepares for every task? Then be that type of employee. Most importantly, be that type of human being.

## CHAPTER SUMMARY

- Preparation is one of the biggest indicators of success.

- When you prepare children, you give them the gift to be able to handle life's obstacles.

- When you are prepared, you show respect and appreciation for others.

# IMPLEMENTATION

Teach your children the importance of preparation by exposing them to many opportunities. The next time you have a project, a meeting, a presentation, or even a get-together, think about ways to show your appreciation by planning well. Find ways to use your attention to detail to show that you really care.

# Presentation

The energy in the air was palpable as hundreds filled the large gymnasium—friends posed for selfies, moms shouted to family members to let them know where they were sitting, grandmothers fanned themselves with programs, and dads set up their video cameras to get just the right angles for their shots. I scrambled to find a seat to watch one of my beloved alumni graduate from high school. I squeezed into a sliver of bleachers between my former student's two proud aunts.

As the valedictorian rose to give his commencement speech, I leaned in, anxious to hear the words he would impart. After all, this was a very reputable high school, and according to the introductory bio that his principal had read about him, this young man's grade point average and academic achievements were nothing short of stellar.

He walked to the podium, shuffled his papers, cleared his throat, looked down, and began: "Um, well, I guess I am living proof that having good grades and high test scores doesn't make someone a good public speaker, but, ummm . . . uh . . . I will try not to make this too painful."

It was all downhill from there. As a courtesy, the audience responded with a smattering of nervous laughter. The once-jolly aunts beside me shifted nervously in their seats and studied their shoes. Several others around me texted on their phones, avoiding eye contact with others in the gym. This brilliant young man made us feel sorry for him, or at the very least, uncomfortable. Throughout the rest of his speech, I couldn't concentrate on his mumbled words as my thoughts fluctuated from pity to sadness to frustration to determination:

> *This poor boy. He is so brilliant, yet he doesn't know how to convey his thoughts to others. He has so much to share, but he doesn't know how to do it!*

> *Why didn't this driven young man practice more so that he would feel more comfortable on such an important day?*

> *How on earth had he reached this stage in his impressive educational journey without anyone helping him work on his presentation skills?*

> *Why hadn't the adults and teachers in his life helped him with this?*

> *How can I encourage other educators to teach their students (and themselves) never ever to apologize when you begin a presentation?*

Let's start with the last point. I am a firm believer in the power and need for an apology when one is warranted, but apologizing for your lack of presentation skills or preparedness is one of the cardinal sins of public speaking. If you apologize for your presentation, it is like saying, "This isn't going to be good. I am wasting your time, but I am going to force you to sit here and listen anyhow!"

Imagine going to a movie theater and settling into your cozy seat with a tub of warm, buttered popcorn and your favorite soda. The screen goes black, and then grandiose music fills the theater as the opening text scrolls across the screen:

> *A long time ago, in a galaxy far, far away,*
> *we had a brilliant idea for a movie.*
> *Unfortunately, we are not good at making movies,*
> *and were nervous while we filmed it,*
> *but we will do our best not to bore you . . .*

Absurd, right? You would get up and leave. Well, you might finish that popcorn first, but then you would go. But every day, someone somewhere stumbles into a presentation with essentially the same words. Please don't be that person. I want more from you. I want more *for* you.

No matter what your profession, at some point most of us have endured excruciating workshops, training sessions, or meetings where the speaker read notes, spoke in a monotone voice, mumbled, or rambled. We all have stories of sitting through PowerPoint lectures with far too many bullet points—and heaven forbid, sound effects—or presenters who did not adequately prepare their content.

To avoid these pitfalls, realize that effective presentations that engage listeners have two equally important components: what you say and how you say it. Here are a few tried-and-true tips to help you refine your presentation skills:

> Realize that effective presentations that engage listeners have two equally important components: what you say and how you say it.

## WHAT YOU SAY

### Storytelling

Effective presenters give facts and information, but they often use the art of storytelling to illustrate their key points. By sharing personal experiences, they effectively weave their information into the presentation in a manner that pulls in the audience members and helps them relate to the information in a more personal way. There is a balance, however. Too many details about minutiae can be overwhelming, and too many personal accounts can be boring or seem narcissistic. One mini narrative to illustrate each key point is sufficient. The stories shouldn't be used to tout oneself; rather, they are used to help the audience relate and connect.

When choosing stories, I have found that stories that I experienced firsthand tend to be more powerful. If you do choose to share something that you have read about elsewhere, it is better if it has not been overused; for example, many of us have heard the story of the starfish (*If I can save just one . . .*) or the story that has been widely shared about the teacher at a dinner party (*What do I make? I make a difference*). They are great stories, which is why they have been widely shared. But find something new, something original. Set yourself apart.

Keep in mind that these tips are more for speeches and formal presentations. In the classroom setting, it is impossible to tell a story for every key idea, but occasionally weave short anecdotes or stories about real-world scenarios into your lessons to connect your students with the content. Just be cautious to avoid becoming that teacher you had who would tell her whole life story and never get to the point. Remember how the kids would laugh about how they got her off topic again so that they didn't have to do the work? Don't be that teacher. Use your time to teach your curricular objective while personalizing your messages in a way that helps your students relate to you and your curriculum.

### Key Messages

Determine a list of key messages that you hope to convey. Are they clear? Are they powerful? Helpful? Would your audience members be able to remember them and relay them to someone else? Here is a trick to consider: If someone in your audience wanted to tweet your key points, quotes, ideas, etc., would it be easy to do?

### Visuals

Not all presentations require visuals, but if you use them, remember that less can be more. Crowded text, small fonts, and blurry photos frustrate your audience. Reading slides aloud can be even worse. Errors in spelling, punctuation, and grammar can lessen your credibility. A few beautiful photos that go with the theme of your message can help keep you on track with your presentation and can be far more memorable than slides filled with too much text and too many photos.

# HOW YOU SAY IT

**Passion**

Imagine this scenario: I take you to a school where you are going to be enrolled in a class all day long, every day, for one week. You will have the same instructor all day from 8:00 a.m. to 3:00 p.m. with only a thirty-minute break for lunch. The school has a long hallway where there are ten different teachers, one of which will be yours.

All ten of the teachers will be following the exact same curriculum. All ten have the exact same lesson plans. All ten of the teachers have the same depth of content knowledge, and they all have the same access to technology and understanding how to implement it and integrate it into their lessons. All ten of the classrooms are even set up, decorated, and designed identically.

When we arrive, I realize that the classes have already begun, and so I ask you, "Would you like to walk up and down the hall, peer into each class for a few minutes, and choose your teacher?" You take me up on the offer, and you peek into each of the ten classrooms for several minutes before making your choice.

If all of the teachers have the same curriculum, lesson plans, content knowledge, technology, and room design, what will you look for? What will make you choose one instructor over another? What will lure you into a classroom and make you say, "That one there—that is the teacher for me!" Think about your answer for a moment.

What did you look for to make your choice? Whenever I have done this exercise with educators or other business professionals, the same answers always rise to the top:

| | |
|---|---|
| *Passion* | *Energy* |
| *Enthusiasm* | *Engagement* |
| *Smiles* | *Relationships* |

Were any of these on your list? For the sake of illustration, let's put all of these under the umbrella of passion. There is a passion for the relationships. There is passion for the content and for how it is being delivered and for how it is being received. Most of us crave to be taught by people who exude passion—an excitement—both for what they are conveying and how they convey it to others. People will often ask me how I choose the people whom I hire to work at the Ron Clark Academy. After all, we have thousands of educators visit each year to observe our classrooms and attend our workshops, so I need to hire extraordinary people. I definitely look for people who have a mastery and understanding of curriculum and instruction. But for me, the passion piece is equally important.

Passion doesn't look the same in every classroom. My classroom is straight down the hallway from Ron Clark's, and our doors face each other. On any given day, I have the privilege of watching him leap on desktops and teach with an animated enthusiasm that engages every child. No one could deny that he has unbridled passion. Also on my hallway is Susan Barnes's classroom. Mrs. Barnes is an artist, an author, and a musician. When she speaks, she weaves her words as only a poet can. She does not jump on desktops like Ron and I do. But her voice has a powerful presence. The cadence of her words and the way she moves draw students into her lessons because she, too, exudes passion. Every teacher in our school has his or her own style, and I intentionally sought out this variety when hiring each of them. I want our students and teachers to realize that passion can take many different forms, but whatever form it takes, when you exude it, people will be drawn to it.

So here is my question for you: If, when you were walking up and down that hallway,

> Passion can take many different forms, but whatever form it takes, when you exude it, people will be drawn to it.

you magically had the ability to peer into your own classroom, would you have chosen it? And if you had yourself as a teacher, what kind of student would you become?

> If you had yourself as a teacher, what kind of student would you become?

If you aren't a teacher, take the same premise and apply it to your work. If you had the ability to watch yourself presenting your ideas in any forum, would you *want* to listen to yourself? Would you choose yourself as a boss? As a coworker?

Most days I would choose my classroom. But if I am honest, some days I would not. Why? Because I am a flawed human, and I am dealing with precious little humans who come with all kinds of wonderful gifts as well as challenges (and hormones). But since I have learned to ask myself that question and honestly answer it, I have become a much better teacher and presenter.

Not every day needs to be a crazy, epic celebration. But if you do not consistently exude a sense of joy or enthusiasm about what you are sharing, how on earth do you expect others to feel that way? If you bore yourself, you certainly cannot be disappointed or hurt when others tune you out. This does not mean that you should change your personality or emulate someone else's—we are all uniquely designed with our own set of gifts, talents, and personality traits. Whatever your personality type, when you show a sense of joy, enthusiasm, passion—even urgency—in your presentations, you engage others at a deeper level.

> Whatever your personality type, when you show a sense of joy, enthusiasm, passion—even urgency—in your presentations, you engage others at a deeper level.

## Body Language

You send subtle (and sometimes not-so-subtle) messages without even speaking a word; for example, I used to have this habit of tilting my head whenever I shook someone's hand for the first time. (Learning to give a good handshake is a mandatory skill at our school.) I had a firm handshake and big smile, but I would bob my head ever so slightly to the right. Subconsciously, I think that I was trying to convey friendliness and warmth. But then a close friend gently shared that tilting my blonde head actually made me look submissive and even ditzy to some. When I lost the head tilt, I still had a friendly handshake, but I came across as more powerful and confident.

Be mindful of your body language and the power of nonverbal communication. I encourage you to read books written by experts in this field to discover what your body language may be saying. Here are a few other things to be aware of regarding your physical communication:

**Movement:** When appropriate, step out from behind the podium. When moving across a stage or a room, move with purpose. Think of your presentation as a research paper. Every time you make a key point to support your thesis, stand still. You may make hand gestures, but plant your feet and weave your words so that your listeners will realize that you are, indeed, making an important point. Then as your words are transitioning to the next point, move to another place in the room. Freeze when you get there to make another key point before moving again. Repeat this throughout your presentation. Avoid pacing back and forth, back and forth. Avoid moving when you are making the key point or telling the climax of the story. Captivate others with the power of your words and voice instead.

**Hands:** Imagine an invisible box in front of you. As you speak, use hand gestures that stay naturally within the box. When you make a key point, move your hands outside the box, thus signaling others that a key message has been delivered. Always avoid putting your hands in your pockets.

**Notes:** Ditch the notes. Avoid reading your presentation. In fact, we have a rule about this at the Ron Clark Academy: Students cannot use notes during a speech—they must learn to speak knowledgeably and from the heart.

**Eye Contact:** When I was young, a teacher told me to look over everyone's heads while giving a speech. If you are terrified in front of an audience, that might be a beginner's survival tactic. But it is far more powerful to look into the eyes of your audience members. Do not stare at one individual for so long that it is uncomfortable, but look from person to person.

If you are a classroom teacher, eye contact is a must. But when you look at a child, please just don't see who they are; believe in what they can become. If you look at a child with disdain or dislike, well, it is better that you

> When you look at a child, please just don't see who they are; believe in what they can become.

not look at all. Children know what you think of them by the way you look at them—they can see it in your eyes. Look with love, compassion, expectation, and belief, even when a child is getting on your last nerve.

## In Smaller Settings

The power of your body language can be magnified in more intimate settings, such as a meeting or a conference. Remember Mr. Halloran? When he spread his feet out under the table and wouldn't move them, he was asserting his dominance loudly and clearly.

If your purpose is to de-escalate a confrontation, then you don't want to appear combative; rather, you want your body language to convey warmth and understanding. Remember the second principle, *motivation*? Your body language should match your motivation. If you are motivated by compassion, let your body language reflect that. If you are motivated by truth, your body language should be that of someone who is listening and who is open to learning others' perspectives.

## BE REAL

For many years, I have worked with a professional speakers' bureau, and this has given me the opportunity to deliver keynote addresses around the world. I am usually hired to impart strategies that empower educators to find better ways to build relationships, increase student engagement, promote academic rigor, and create a climate and culture for success. This has always been the case, yet my methods and style have definitely evolved with experience.

Almost twenty years ago, before working for the speakers' bureau, I gave my first keynote speech to a large audience of educators. I took the microphone and read my remarks with great enthusiasm. I was prepared. I was eloquent. I was intelligent. I was polished.

At lunch, I asked a trusted colleague if my remarks were okay. He gently looked at me and said, "Kim, you were poised and smart and you did a good job, but the person in front of that room was not the person I know. The Kim I know is funny and warm and a little goofy. It is great to be polished, but if you will let people see the person your friends and students know, you will really be a force to be reckoned with!"

Tears filled my eyes because his words stung, but also because there was truth in them. I had always thought that there needed to be a formality and polish to my presentations. To be clear, professionalism is important. But you must also let your personality—who you really are—shine through. I didn't just want to be a speaking mannequin with all the right words. I wanted to be someone who connected with people on a stage the same way that I was able to do in day-to-day life. I began to find ways to share both my expertise and my personality, but it would be about five more years before I learned how to connect on an entirely different level.

I was booked to give a speech to a school district in the western part of the United States. Prior to the engagement, the superintendent asked for a phone conference. As he spoke, I was immediately struck by both his candor and his passion for kids; I also admired how much he supported his team. He told me that budget cuts had forced his teachers to do more with less, be more for their students, and give more of themselves than ever before; additionally, he knew that several of his teachers were facing financial ruin, family problems, and other challenges in their personal lives that were making it increasingly harder for them to function in their classrooms. He was worried about employee burnout and the effects that it would have on his students. If you are an educator, this kind of scenario probably sounds all too familiar.

His request was simple: "Look, Kim, I don't know if you can relate to the types of personal challenges that my faculty and staff are facing, but if there is some way that you can weave them into your presentation, I think that it would mean the world to them, and it would help my students. My teachers are good—they know what they are supposed to do. I fear that some of them just don't have it in them anymore to do what they need to do."

His insight moved me. Here I had been going from state to state telling teachers *what* they needed to do, but I had not been showing them *how* on earth it could be possible. The absolute irony was that I had the ability to address his concerns. I had overcome many challenges in my personal life, and I had learned how to take my adversity and turn it into fulfillment. Why hadn't I ever shared my story before? I thought I was healed, but was I still embarrassed by it?

The conversation with that superintendent was a major turning point on my speaking path, and it completely altered my approach to inspiring and motivating others to achieve. I gave the speech he had requested. I told my story publicly for the first time, and I held nothing back from a crowd of complete strangers; I allowed myself to be completely vulnerable. I was terrified. I feared judgment. But the audience embraced my message—they laughed and they cried. Most importantly, they listened. They really heard what I said, and they understood how to take their own pain and turn it into something positive in their own classrooms. As I packed up my things, a line of teachers formed. Most just wanted a hug. They thanked me for being real, acknowledging their struggles, and reminding them of their purpose. My heart felt full.

Afterward, as I was walking to my rental car, I heard someone calling my name. I looked up to see a middle-aged woman running across the parking lot. She approached me with tears in her weary eyes. "I needed to talk to you," she said, her voice catching. "I needed to say 'thank you.' Your story is my story, and now I know that I can do this. I can go on."

I simply hugged her, and I held her for several moments. She had no idea, but she was helping me, too—she was validating me and filling my heart with appreciation for what I had learned that day. We talked for a while after that, and she shared that she had been teaching for twenty-five years. She knew she was a good teacher, but in the midst of dealing with so much pain in her personal life, she felt like she couldn't be there for the kids. She had been thinking about leaving the profession and moving far away. She realized that day that she did belong in her classroom after all and that she could be there for her students.

Since that experience, I have delivered hundreds more speeches. And each time I enjoy the blessing of speaking, I learn something new, and I pray that I am able to relate to the members of my audience like they are dear old friends. I do not mean to imply that every time you do a presentation, you have to talk about your business and share your personal drama. Not every situation is appropriate for that kind of intimacy. But if you are asking others to do more, be more, or engage more, providing a little food for the soul can certainly help. Acknowledge when things are hard. Be vulnerable, not apologetic. Share your triumphs and your flaws and talk about what you've learned along the way. Think about it: Do you choose your friends because they are polished and perfect, or because they are real? Perfection is boring. Authenticity is what is truly appealing.

> Perfection is boring. Authenticity is what is truly appealing.

Every one of us will experience difficult circumstances at different seasons in our lives—marital discord, financial struggles, health issues, concerns for our children or our parents—the list goes on. These challenges become roadblocks that can create negativity, bitterness, sadness, a sense of failure, and even despair. They can leave us feeling ordinary, broken, and forgotten. If we take this into consideration when presenting and strive to help others as a part of our motivation, our words can have tremendous power. There is joy and meaning surrounding us all, no matter how difficult the circumstances. If we can help others recognize this and seize hold of it, we are able to give far more than a presentation; we are able to give hope.

## CHAPTER SUMMARY

- Apologizing for a presentation makes the audience uncomfortable and lessens your credibility.
- Presentations are affected by two components: what you say and how you say it.
- Storytelling, key messages, and visuals can have an impact upon what you say.
- Body language, eye contact, and movement can affect how you say it.
- Passion and enthusiasm will draw others to your message.
- Authenticity is far more appealing than perfection.

## IMPLEMENTATION

The next time you give a presentation, practice and prepare using the tools for what you say and how you say it. Most importantly, show your audience who you really are. The connection that they make with you will affect the connection they make with your content.

# Reconciliation

I was running late that Monday morning, and I struggled to find my ringing phone as I unwound myself from an impossible tangle of book bags. (Yes, I am one of those teachers who thinks that if she carries ungraded papers around long enough, fairies and gnomes will magically grade them in the middle of the night.) I freed myself just before the call went to voicemail. The mother of one of my students was on the other end. "Hi, Mrs. Bearden. This is Mrs. Long, Tara's mother. I am sorry to bother you. I know I don't have an appointment and that you are about to start your day, but can I possibly come in and talk to you for a few minutes? I am still in the parking lot, and I need some advice."

Normally, I would have suggested that we schedule a time when things weren't so rushed, but by the crackle in her voice, I could tell she was on the verge of tears. "Sure. Come on in the building. I will meet you in the lobby," I responded.

"Is it okay if I check in at the desk and just come to your room?" she asked. "Tara thinks that I left after I dropped her off, and she will be even more upset with me if she knows I got you involved."

She piqued my curiosity with that comment, and I agreed. A few minutes later, Mrs. Long entered my office, took a seat, put her face in her hands, and sighed. She looked as though she wanted to fade into the chair; her exhaustion was evident.

"How can I help you, Mrs. Long? Please let me know what is on your heart and mind," I said.

Mrs. Long shared how her household had turned into World War III due to her constant arguing and bickering with her daughter. Her daughter had become challenging, sullen, withdrawn, and even disrespectful. None of these descriptors fit the lovely little girl that I knew so well, but I had noticed a sadness in Tara recently, and we all know that parents often have the distinct privilege of seeing their own children at their very worst.

Mrs. Long said that every day was an argument and that the past weekend had been unbearable. The slightest request for Tara to do homework or to clean her room was met with eye rolling and lip smacking. "I don't even like my own daughter anymore. I love her, but I want nothing to do with her right now. I don't even know who she is. The whole thing makes me feel like a horrible mother."

After thanking Mrs. Long for trusting me with her frustrations and reassuring her that she was, in fact, a wonderful mother, I offered to help. "Well, something is definitely going on with her," I said. "Do you mind if I talk with her to get some insight? I have a strong connection with Tara, so she won't find it odd if I sit down with her and mention that I have noticed that she has seemed unhappy lately."

"Well, okay. Thank you. But please don't tell her I was in here complaining about her."

"I've got this," I said. "I will call you later to follow up." Mrs. Long hugged me tightly and left.

Later that day, I purposefully planted myself outside of Tara's classroom so that I could catch her walking by. She smiled when she saw me, and I said, "Tara, can you come with me for a minute?"

"Yes, ma'am," she replied.

As we sat in my office, I started, "Sweetie, you aren't in any kind of trouble. I have just noticed that you seem a little sad. Is everything okay?"

"Yes, ma'am. I'm fine," she answered while pulling the palms of her hands into her sweatshirt sleeves. She picked at her chipped fingernail polish.

"Tara, I am glad you are fine, but I would like for you to be better than fine. How are things going at school? Has there been any drama?"

She looked up. "No, ma'am. School is good."

"How about home?" I asked. I watched as a single tear spilled out of her left eye and rolled down her cheek. She quickly reached to wipe it away, but it was too late—she knew I had seen it.

"Baby, what is it? Talk to me. How can I help?" I asked.

She replied, "Why can't things just be like they used to be? Why can't we go back to the way things were?"

"Who?" I asked. "Who is 'we?'"

"My mom and my dad. They just yell at me all the time, and so I yell back. They are always fussing about my homework, my grades, my room, my laundry."

"Well, do you think they have a reason to fuss? Are you carrying through on your responsibilities?" I asked while gently pushing her bangs out of her eyes.

"Well, no. I guess I could do better. But they just make me so mad. I don't even care anymore. They are always nagging. I can tell that they don't like me very much, and I don't like them very much, either."

If you have had any dealings with a middle school girl, you recognize that this conversation was pretty much a standard one: Child is hormonal and disrespectful; parent fusses; child responds negatively; parent fusses more and gives consequences; child responds horribly. It is a cycle that continues for a good four to six years in some households.

I continued, "Tara, please complete this sentence. Things would be so much better if . . . "

I waited. She finally responded, "Things would be so much better if we would watch movies together like we used to and if we would play board games like we used to."

"So, what you really want is time with your parents?" I asked.

"Yes. Without them fussing at me," she added.

"Mind if I tell them?" I asked.

"It doesn't matter," she answered, but I knew that it did.

Later that day I called Mrs. Long and explained the conversation.

"I am so confused," she said. "Tara slams her door and avoids us, but she told you she wants time with us? I'm not buying it."

"Look, I hear you," I said. "I raised a teenage daughter, and I have taught hundreds of teenage girls. But stick with me here. I have an idea. I realize that Tara has not been carrying through on her commitments—she even admits it. I also understand that there should be consequences and that she deserves to be corrected. But can I make a suggestion?"

"At this point, I have nothing to lose," Mrs. Long responded.

"Exactly. If this doesn't work, you can try something else. Here is my idea: What if you all agree to designate a fuss-free family time every Saturday afternoon, and the time is spent at home playing games, watching movies, and just being together? There have to be ground rules for all of you: no talking about grades, no talking about cleaning the room, no talking about what Tara has or hasn't done. You have to put all of that aside from noon to four every Saturday afternoon, no matter what. Laugh together, play together, get back to the way it used to be, despite Tara's lack of responsibility. Don't do anything extravagant or expensive—stay at home or go to the park. Keep it simple. After that window has passed, you can require her to clean her room, do homework, anything. But noon to four on Saturday afternoon is sacred family time."

> What if you all agree to designate a fuss-free family time every Saturday afternoon, and the time is spent at home playing games, watching movies, and just being together?

"Do you really think it will work?" she asked.

"Yes, I think that you all have drifted so far away from the bonds that you once had that you are now pushing each other even further away. And look at the positives here—your daughter has said that she actually longs for time with you. Explain the rules to Tara. Tell her that although you are not happy about some issues, you still love her very much and you want to spend time with her like you used to do."

"Okay, we will try it," she said.

The next Monday morning, both Mrs. Long and Tara entered the school arm in arm, huge smiles on their faces. They both hugged me in the lobby.

"We have reconciled," shared Mrs. Long.

"Yep, we had a truce," shared Tara. "Thank you, Mrs. Bearden, for giving me my mom back!" she said as she skipped off to class.

Mrs. Long hugged me again and filled me in. "We had stopped listening and laughing together. We had forgotten how much we could enjoy each other! We watched movies, and Tara put her head in my lap like she did as a little girl. I stroked her hair, and she fell asleep. I just stared at her and remembered all the reasons that I love her. When she awoke, we made spaghetti and cookies together, and we laughed and laughed when we beat her dad at UNO. It was actually about 7:00 that evening when I hesitantly asked Tara if she wouldn't mind cleaning her room. She hugged me, said she would be glad to, and bounced up the stairs to do it. I couldn't believe it."

Since the Long's fuss-free family time, I have given the same recommendation, or variations of it, to countless families so that they, too, could reconcile with one another and start anew.

I once had a sweet, wonderful mother who complained that her son never listened to her. Upon further inquiry, I learned that every single morning, this mother spent the entire car ride to school telling the child what he needed to do that day in order to be successful. For thirty minutes she talked nonstop. Every day. "What do I need to do to make him listen to me?" she implored.

My answer: "Stop talking. Hush. Do not say a single word on the way to school, other than 'Good morning' and 'Have a nice day.'"

"But I am trying to tell him what he needs to do," she protested.

"Look, Mama," I responded, "don't you think that he already knows what to do?"

"Well, yes," she said, "but he is not doing it."

"That is because you are nagging the life out of him. He is rebelling. I beg you—do not speak for the next three days. Just be cheerful and kind and wish him well."

Guess what happened after three days? The child initiated conversation and even asked to be quizzed on vocabulary on the way to school.

This is not a book about parenting, and I certainly realize that many relationships and family issues are far more complex. And to be clear, we are one of the strictest middle schools in the country; I believe in high expectations, rules, and consequences. The key point is that when the relationship is broken, *reconciliation* must occur in order to move forward and make progress.

I love all of my students; I am wired that way. If I am honest with you, though, I must admit that I don't always like all of them. Whenever I find myself nagging and fussing incessantly at a child, I focus on the first principle, *consideration*, and this helps me operate with a desire for reconciliation. If I am unable to develop a rapport with a child, my inability to connect with him or her can have a negative effect on my ability to discipline with positive results. Sometimes, as teachers, we go out of our way to avoid those kids who get on our nerves. That is human nature; however, I challenge you try the opposite approach. Go out of your way to spend time with those kids instead. Eat lunch with them, chat with them in the hallways, even go watch them play ball. By getting to know a child outside of class, you are more able to effectively reconcile the relationship and build a rapport inside the class. It always works for me.

## FORGIVENESS: ASK FOR IT AND OFFER IT

Sometimes we must take into consideration that we are completely wrong and need to apologize. We all have bad days—moments when we wish that we could take back our words, make a different choice, and have a do-over. But life doesn't work that way, so the best we can do is sincerely apologize for our mistakes or shortcomings. Even if you are not the only one at fault, an apology is still necessary.

You may think that "I'm sorry" is a sign of weakness, but offering an apology and admitting fault takes courage; it takes strength of character.

*I am sorry that I was impatient with you.*

*I was distracted earlier, and I apologize for not stopping to listen.*

*I realize that I hurt you. I hope that you will accept my sincere apology.*

*I was wrong, and I hope you will accept my apology for my part in all of this.*

*I am sorry. How can I make this up to you?*

Reconciliation also requires us to forgive. Sometimes the walls we have built are so thick that "fuss-free time" is impossible; we need those walls to protect ourselves from what is on the other side of them. I have the opportunity to interact with thousands of educators each year, and I am often blessed to hear their stories. Many will share their personal tragedies and challenges with me, and the pain and heartache some have had to face is incomprehensible. We all know that there are some who have been given burdens that we will truly never understand until we meet our Maker; however, I have found that those individuals who cannot move beyond the pain, despite their horrific circumstances, usually stay stuck because someone did something to them. They were hurt, betrayed, or damaged by someone else, and the anger and anguish festered within them. I know

> Offering forgiveness to another is the greatest gift you can give yourself.

that I can never fully understand the sorrow that some people have endured and that forgiveness is not easy.

Yet here is an important truth: The person you need to forgive doesn't have to deserve or earn your forgiveness. If and when you are able to do so, offering forgiveness to another is the greatest gift you can give yourself. Why? Because no longer does that person have control over your happiness, and you are free to live. Forgiveness releases the control that the other person has over you.

Forgiveness takes time, and it may even require that you do it in stages. Sometimes you don't even need to communicate with the person you are forgiving; to do so might be too painful or even too dangerous. But within your heart, if you are able to forgive, your soul will begin to heal. You will find a way to use your story to help others who have been hurt, and this will help you make meaning and find purpose in the midst of your pain. If your anguish can be reconciled within your soul, you will be released from the chains that have bound you. I wish this for all the souls who are lost and hurting. I wish this for you.

## CHAPTER SUMMARY

- Broken relationships need reconciliation in order to re-establish rapport.

- Quality time together can be a powerful way to reconnect.

- When we have wronged another, we must learn to apologize.

- Forgiveness is difficult, but when you are able to do it, it releases the other person's control over you.

## IMPLEMENTATION

If you have a challenging relationship, try finding ways to spend quality time with one another. If you need to apologize, do so. If someone has wronged you, work on finding forgiveness. It is a gift you give yourself.

# Confrontation

With our newly expanded family and their ever-expanding shoe sizes, we quickly filled every nook and cranny of our house. Skateboards, shin guards, basketballs, and backpacks became our new décor, and although we loved our home, we entertained the idea of looking at other housing options, just to see what was available.

I spent a few summer Sundays attending open houses for homes on the market. Most of the options did not meet the criteria for our budget—we had recently adopted our three teenage boys from Soweto, South Africa, who could eat more food than I thought humanly possible.

One particular Sunday, Sisipho and Sabelo (two of my three boys) decided to tag along with me to check out a house that intrigued us online. It was over our budget, but the thought of four bedrooms and a basement made it worth a look. After swimming at a friend's pool, I threw my wet hair into a ponytail, put on an old sundress, and piled the boys into our dented SUV.

As we pulled up to the house, a gleaming Lexus simultaneously pulled up behind us, reminding me how badly I needed to wash our car. Two striking black women emerged from the vehicle. Both were impeccably dressed in vibrant prints and wore their hair in long, flowing locks. They smiled, nodded, and said, "Hello," and we fell in line behind them to enter the home.

Once inside, two twenty-something, bouncy blonde real estate agents leapt to attention from the kitchen table where they were sorting flyers. I noted that one of them looked like a significantly younger version of me. They anxiously greeted the other women, blocking their entrance into the living room.

"Oh, um . . . hello. Are you here for the open house?"

*Isn't that kind of obvious?* I wondered as I stood behind them.

The black women nodded and smiled yes.

"Oh, okay. Um . . . have you been preapproved for a loan?" said realtor number one as realtor number two quickly followed up with, "How much have you been approved for?"

*Huh?* That was new. I hadn't been asked that at any open houses I had attended unless I had expressed a real interest in the home. *Okay, Kim. You are being overly sensitive. They are going to ask you the same thing,* I thought to myself.

Only they didn't. In fact, they looked past the women and past my sons (whom they assumed were not with me) as I stepped out from behind Sisipho.

Noticing me for the first time, realtor number one beamed and smiled broadly. "Oh, hello! We didn't see you here! Please make yourself at home and let us know if you have any questions!" they both exuberantly exclaimed, faces alight with the anticipation of a possible sale. Just like that, I was greeted with smiles, giggles, and an invitation to roam without so much as a handshake.

Dumbfounded, I grabbed my boys' hands. "Sisipho, Sabelo, come with me!" I said. The shock on the realtors' faces was evident when they realized the boys and I were together. I darted through a door to my closest escape—a stairwell to the upstairs bedroom. As we ascended the steps, I could hear the women continue to explain that no, they hadn't been approved, but that they were just starting to look at homes. The blatant interrogation continued until we were out of earshot.

Once inside the bedroom, I huffed, I puffed, I paced. *What do I do? What do I say?* Sisipho, somewhat dumbfounded, asked, "What is wrong? Why are you so upset?"

"I am angry," I replied, clenching my fists. "Let's go."

"So, we are not going to look at the house?" asked Sabelo.

Not wanting to make a scene, I snapped, "Yes, let's look." My demeanor completely confused them. Disbelief and confusion welled inside me as I numbly wandered from room to room. Was I overreacting? Was I just being hypersensitive? I wanted that to be the case. I am a very rational person, and in my gut, I sensed that I was not being irrational—I was being perceptive.

Once inside our car, Sisipho asked me again what on earth was wrong. "Are you okay? Why are you so upset?"

Sighing, I placed my head on the steering wheel while tears filled my eyes. Do I tell them why? Do I explain to them that this is a reality? Do I break their hearts, or do I say nothing? And if I say something, do I turn them into angry, disillusioned young men? How on earth do I teach them to continue to love all people while still making them aware that not all people will love them? Some will judge them, and others will even hate them without knowing their hearts or their souls, simply because of their skin. How do I tell them this? And as these thoughts sped through my head, my mind was flooded with countless faces of my students' mamas, and I wanted to weep for them, for their sons, for my sons, and for our world.

Finally, I lifted my head and shifted in my seat to face them both. Looking them straight in the eyes, I said, "That, my dear sons, was white privilege. When you hear others talking about it, you now know what it looks like. Those two black women were continuously interrogated about why they were there and were asked if they were approved for a loan, yet I bounced in with my wet hair and flip-flops and the assumption was made that I had every right to be there and that I could, of course, buy that house."

Silence.

"Oh," said Sisipho, lowering his head.

And a little piece of my heart broke.

"I am angry with myself, too," I continued. "I said nothing. I should have said, 'Aren't you going to ask me if I have been preapproved, too, just like you asked these lovely women?' But I didn't. I remained silent. And for that, I am sorry and ashamed."

Unfortunately, I have witnessed countless situations where this same scenario has played out. Each story has different characters and different settings, but the plot remains constant. Still, I argued with myself that it is standard for realtors to ask if someone is preapproved. I know that. But I wasn't asked. If anyone didn't have a right to be there, it was I. I had no intention of buying that house. I just wanted to look at it and dream a little; however, the assumption was made that I belonged there.

Those bouncy blonde realtors did nothing illegal. It could be argued that they were professional and polite; they might have even followed their company protocol. But they were relentless in their interrogation of the other women.

I hate conflict. I am known as a kind of teacher who is armed with hugs and smiles, laughter and joy. The thought of confronting someone else used to create an anxiety within me that made me want to run and hide. But there comes a time in life when we must decide if we want to exist for ourselves or live for others—a time when we understand that sometimes we must fight for what is right. In such instances, *confrontation* is both warranted and necessary.

> But there comes a time in life when we must decide if we want to exist for ourselves or live for others—a time when we understand that sometimes we must fight for what is right.

In the case of the realtors, I was upset and angry, and the mama bear in me wanted to protect my young. Instead of handling it rationally, however, I did nothing at all. But the next time that I found myself in a similar situation, I was ready. Well, almost ready.

It was a beautiful Saturday, and my son Sabelo and I had been laughing all morning as we ran errands around town. Our last stop was his scheduled eye exam. We entered the large vision center and signed in.

The receptionist greeted us robotically, and then she looked at my son's name, Sabelo Hlatshwayo, on the clipboard.

"Oh, my! What on earth? What a very strange name!" she blurted loudly.

Taken aback, my usually charming and engaging son stared at her blankly and blinked. My jaw dropped.

I swallowed and said, "He is adopted from South Africa."

My Zulu son comes from a culture where names have great meaning, and he takes great pride in his. Different isn't "strange." Different is beautiful. I wanted to say this, but I was offended. I said nothing else. Epic fail. Again.

So how did I make it right this time? I took Sabelo home after his appointment and stewed. And prayed. And then I turned around and drove the twenty minutes back to the vision center again. I calmly walked in, reached across the counter, took the receptionist's hand in mine, and said, "Hi. I was here earlier with my son. Do you remember me?" She nodded and gave me an obligatory smile.

I continued, "I felt led to come back here. There are some things I really want and need you to understand. Can I share them with you?" Wide-eyed, she nodded again.

I shared the importance of my child's name to his Zulu heritage. I explained that her words were hurtful to him. I shared that it is okay to say a name is unique or even to ask more about it, but never to call it strange. I asked her to consider this whenever she meets someone who is different than she, especially a child. She listened intently and nodded. She teared up. She apologized profusely. She thanked me for making her aware and for taking the time to come back and talk to her in a kind way. She said she never wanted to be seen as someone who doesn't care about all people. I nodded and validated that I believed her because she had taken the time to listen and receive what I was saying. I thanked her for her time and understanding, gave her hand a final squeeze, and left.

When I got home, I explained to Sabelo what I had done. He was both shocked and grateful that I had gone back. "You didn't have to do that for me," he said.

"Oh, yes, I did, sweetie. I needed to confront her in hopes that I could help her understand. It doesn't always work out as well as it did today, but I should not be afraid to say what needs to be said." My experiences with my beloved sons have taught me no longer to fear speaking truth even when it is difficult to do so.

## THE DANGER OF PLACATION

In an effort to avoid confrontation, we sometimes choose to placate others just to keep the peace. Placation is exhausting and unhealthy, especially when trying to mold children into responsible adults.

"Mommy loves you so much, but it makes Mommy sad when she has to come in for a conference like this," Mrs. Kirby said in a lilting voice while rubbing her son Max's back. Meanwhile, baby brother ran around my room like his hair had been set on fire. "Mommy doesn't like it when you run! Please stop," she whined. Baby brother paid her no mind and continued his running.

"So, Maxie, is it true that you were unkind? I find that hard to believe. Can you tell me why you felt like you needed to be unkind? Did someone hurt your feelings?" Max rolled his eyes and pulled away.

I wanted to roll my eyes, too, as I listened to the exchange between Mrs. Kirby and her eleven-year-old hellion, Max. Max was spoiled, mean, and a challenge, to say the least. I took into consideration that there might be more to the story, but I also witnessed that Max needed some good old-fashioned discipline, something his mother was obviously reluctant to give. Whenever I saw Max interact with his mother, the exchange was the same. She didn't seem to comprehend why her precious baby boy needed consequences. After all, consequences made her little Maxie sad, and his sadness made her feel sad, too.

Max was disrespectful to his mother, too, and whenever he was, she would continue in her pleading voice to placate him. I couldn't decide if she was oblivious to his disrespect or if she was afraid of him. I did know that Max was her whole world, and somehow her devotion had blinded her. She failed to realize that Max's momentary happiness might cause him tremendous unhappiness down the road if he didn't learn how to accept responsibility for his actions and treat people with kindness. Either way, he ruled his household, and the whole situation was unhealthy for Max, his mother, and his baby brother.

I had to work with that mother throughout the school year to guide her how to say "no" and enforce consequences. I also had many a talk with Max to teach him that while he had been allowed to display disrespectful behaviors in his past, we would not tolerate them at our school. The whole thing wore me down, but I knew that it was best for Max and his whole family to stay the course.

We have all known children—and adults—whose behaviors are so unpleasant that they exhaust everyone around them. And too often, we just placate them as a result. We say what they want to hear and do what they want us to do just to keep the peace. When we do this with children, we teach them that there are not consequences for their actions; we lead them to believe that the world does, indeed, revolve around them. With adults, it can be even more unpleasant. But when we choose placation instead of confrontation, no one benefits.

As we guide children, there are many times when we must confront their behaviors. We can do so without making the confrontation a humiliating experience. When angry or frustrated students are metaphorically backed into a corner while being disciplined, they will sometimes respond defensively or negatively. In such cases, private confrontation is always much more effective than public humiliation. Speak quietly to the child alone, talk to the student after class. Make choices that de-escalate the situation rather than escalate it.

## DEALING WITH CONFLICT

What if you have a conflict or concern with a coworker, parent, or even a friend? It is always best to go right to the person on your own and speak with him or her politely and truthfully. Use the six principles to guide you as you share your frustrations or concerns. And for heaven's sake, do not tell your concerns to everyone else in your organization—give the person the benefit of the doubt and speak to him or her directly.

It is okay to seek out guidance from a mentor or trusted advisor, and if things don't go well during your initial meeting, it is helpful to get a supervisor to mediate. But if you talk to everyone else before addressing an issue with the individual who is directly involved, you are really looking for attention, not advice. You are stirring up drama, not creating solutions. In the end, the other party still might not respond to your concerns as you would have liked, but leading with *consideration, motivation,* and even *validation* can certainly help things go more smoothly. Here are a few ways to start those potentially difficult conversations:

> If you talk to everyone else before addressing an issue with the individual who is directly involved, you are really looking for attention, not advice.

*Can we talk? I am feeling uneasy about something, and I want to come to you with my concerns.*

*Something is heavy on my heart, and I would appreciate it if we could clear the air.*

*I appreciate you stopping by. Can we talk about something that is causing me some frustration?*

*You are a good friend, and so I would like to talk to you about something that has left me feeling hurt.*

*When you made that comment, I felt confused. Can you help me understand where you were coming from?*

*Can I share how I feel about this situation so that we can find a solution that works for both of us?*

*I know that your intentions were good, but when you dropped the ball on this, you really left me in a bind.*

*I am sensing tension between us, and so I was wondering if we could talk about it.*

*I am willing to help you in any way that I can, but lately I feel frustrated with your lack of commitment to the team.*

Many years ago, I had to fire a teacher for poor job performance. Firing someone is a horrendous task, and to make things worse, she was a lovely person. She just wasn't cut out for teaching. I lay awake the night before, consumed with dread as I carefully considered the message I hoped to convey. This woman didn't have the skills to teach, but she did have many wonderful qualities, and I made a point of writing them down. The next morning, I mentioned those qualities when I told her all of the good things I saw within her. I noted her love for children and shared other ideas I had for ways she could still work with them in another capacity. After her dismissal, she sent me an email: "Although you let me go, I want to thank you for doing it in a way that gave me dignity and validated my worth. You managed to make me feel valued, even though I wasn't the right fit for the position. I am extremely grateful to you for that." This lovely woman might not have been suited to be a teacher, but she definitely taught me that even extremely unpleasant confrontations can be made less painful when they are tempered with consideration and validation.

Sometimes confrontations don't go smoothly and you might just have to agree to disagree. Sometimes you might have to stand your ground to fight for what is right. Sometimes you might have to walk away. But if you begin with the six principles, you can rest assured that in the very least, you have handled the situation with honor and grace.

## CHAPTER SUMMARY

- Confrontation is difficult, but sometimes it is necessary.
- If you are too emotional about an issue, wait until you are calmer to confront it.
- Placation can be more harmful than confrontation.
- Confrontation doesn't need to be hateful or mean spirited.
- Confrontation can provide others with insight that they did not previously have.
- If the confrontation does not go well, find peace in how you conducted yourself.

## IMPLEMENTATION

The next time you have a situation that requires confrontation, think through how you will express your points using the six principles. Even write out your points beforehand if necessary. Try to temper your emotions, and as always, take the other person's perspective into consideration.

# 11

# Separation

My prayers had been answered, and we were finally able to move out of the house that I had occupied for seventeen years. It had once been a happy home, but after the arguments, the betrayal, the sadness, and the pain, my former sanctuary had been transformed into a place where bad memories held me captive. Wherever I looked, I saw tainted memories, and I wanted to get rid of every evidence of the pain.

That difficult chapter of my life had long been closed. I had learned to trust again and had since married the great love of my life, my husband Scotty; however, so many of the items in the house felt like constant reminders of the past that I couldn't escape, despite my newfound joy. When I married Scotty, he moved into the house with my daughter Madison and me. Scotty did his best to spruce up the things that had fallen into disrepair both during my previous marriage and when I had been a struggling single mom. With Madison out on her own, it was finally time to put the house on the market.

The first order of business was a huge moving sale. And by huge, I mean that we lined our driveway, garage, and yard with every single piece of furniture and décor from inside that house. I only spared our clothes, photographs, and the new bed we bought when we married. Scotty, ever supportive, simply shrugged and said, "If that is what you want to do, honey." The sale was to start at 8:00 a.m., but by 7:30, cars were already lining the street.

By 4:00 that afternoon, although we had sold a large portion of the items, many still remained. Dressers, mirrors, tables, lamps, a buffet, and chairs littered my yard; pillows, comforters, and abandoned housewares were strewn about. Scotty started to haul everything back into the house, and I stopped him. "Scotty, we just can't take it back inside. Please don't."

"Honey, I know you don't want it anymore, but we need to figure out a place to put it in the meantime."

"Can't we just give it all away?" I asked.

"Okay, honey. That is fine. Maybe I can rent a truck next week and we can take it to the Goodwill."

Just as I was deciding if that felt like the answer, a young family pulled up with a pickup truck to get the couch and loveseat they had purchased earlier that day. Instantly, I knew what do.

"Let's give it all to them!" I said. Scotty nodded as a smile spread across his face.

As they approached, I said, "Would you like the rest of it?" as I pointed to it all.

"Oh, no, thank you. We have no money left," said the young mother. She held the hands of two toddlers; another baby was on the way.

"No, I don't want you to pay for it. I am going to give it to you. You can have it all if you want it!"

There were some language barriers between us, but I knew the moment when she finally understood. Tears pooled in her eyes. She threw her arms around me, and then she hugged her husband. Within minutes, she made several phone calls. Forty-five minutes later, eight pickup trucks pulled up and took away every last remnant of my former life. I had no furniture left, except for a bed.

I had never felt richer or more at peace.

Scotty and I took our garage sale earnings and bought some modest new furnishings at IKEA. We moved into a tiny, two-bedroom rental house near my school. *I loved it.* We stayed there until the next set of miracles—our three sons—arrived.

## A CLEAN BREAK

Just like I needed to free myself from that stuff so that I could move forward, we sometimes need to separate ourselves from people, too. The reality is that, in some situations, no matter how many strategies you use and no matter how noble you are, relationships do not work. They may even be downright unhealthy or even unsafe, and in those cases, the best thing you can do is let go. Completely.

In the professional world, we often have no choice but to engage with challenging individuals. It is not realistic to say, "Avoid all negative people." We can't. The six principles are designed to help make dealing with those misery evangelists a little easier, but I don't want to sell you a false bill of goods. If you have honestly tried the six principles and have conducted yourself with complete professionalism without making any headway, seek out the assistance of a supervisor or another coworker who can mediate or handle the situation on your behalf.

Now, if it is a student who is testing your patience, you cannot give up or walk away. You must find ways to reconcile, build a relationship, and seek to understand. Adults should know better, though, so if there is someone who continually belittles you, harms you, hurts you, or makes you feel like you are insignificant despite your efforts to communicate effectively, find a way to get distance from him or her. Be intentional about surrounding yourself with people who fuel your soul, not those who deplete it.

> Be intentional about surrounding yourself with people who fuel your soul, not those who deplete it.

Your life has great purpose, and if another's hatred or negativity wounds your soul and pulls you from that purpose, it is time for you to graciously and gracefully walk away from that relationship. Perhaps you should spend less time with the person. Perhaps you should completely disengage. You can wish them well on their journey, but let your journey take a different path.

## CHAPTER SUMMARY

- Sometimes, despite our best efforts, it is better to end a relationship.
- If you are struggling with a professional relationship, try the six principles first.
- You mustn't give up on children; find ways to get help when dealing with them.
- If you are in a dangerous or unhealthy situation, you must completely disengage.

## IMPLEMENTATION

If you find yourself in a situation where you have to interact with a difficult person, first try to handle it using the six principles. If you are in need of support, seek out a mentor or supervisor. If the relationship is toxic or if you feel belittled or unsafe, end the relationship. You deserve better.

## chapter 12

# Pontification

The following is part of a text exchange with my former student, Osei:

**Me:** Dost thou desire to partake in an exchange of utterances?

**Osei:** Indubitably. I am beholden to thee for the impartation of thine erudition.

**Me:** Thou art the shrewdest scholar under my tutelage.

**Osei:** Thou dost adulate me servilely. Nonetheless, I beseech thee to sustain thy encomiums.

**Me:** I dost not desire to inspire a proclivity for haughtiness!

**Osei:** I shall remain obsequious!

**Me:** Admirable. Now commence with thy cogitation concerning thy onus.

**Osei:** Fie! Yes, ma'am. I will do my homework now! ☺ Goodnight!

Osei loves words and the power they possess. This game, which we regularly played, sprung from a conversation about *pontification* (another word Osei liked). When you pontificate, you pompously use language to impress with little regard to how your words will actually connect with others or convey your message. I am like Osei—I am fascinated with the English language, and I am constantly working to increase my vocabulary. That said, it pains us all to read or listen to someone who obviously uses words just to try to prove intelligence. Simply put, speak simply.

Whether you're using the spoken or the written word, you must know your audience and choose words that will draw them in, not perplex them. "But I want to educate people and encourage them to increase their vocabulary!" you might say. Well, good for you. But if they are adults, that is not your job. If they are kids, it is. But increasing one's vocabulary does not mean that you have to use every difficult word you know when having a conversation. Doing so may even backfire and make you appear to be insecure or arrogant. Irregardless, you must conversate effectively to gain the trust of others. (And if you thought that the last sentence seemed incorrect, you were right. *Irregardless* and *conversate* are both considered nonstandard English, like *ain't*.) The message here is if you are going to use large words, do so correctly.

Arrogance isn't just demonstrated through the use of difficult words; it is also displayed through simple language laced with bravado. Confidence is attractive; arrogance is not. Those who speak with confidence are assertive and knowledgeable. They are also open to receiving, learning, and growing. Arrogant people think they know far more than the rest of us. They miss the truth that knowledge is not the same as wisdom. The wise understand that until we die, there is always more to learn. Sometimes, arrogance is really a mask for insecurity; sometimes it truly is narcissism. In either case, I have never known anyone who finds it appealing.

> Confidence is attractive; arrogance is not.

**Confident Language**

*I will be happy to help with that project. I have experience in this area, and I think I can be of help.*

*I have learned some things, and I would love to share them with the team.*

*Yes, this will be a challenge, but I am willing and able to rise to the occasion! I won't let you down.*

*Thank you for your suggestions. I am always looking for ways to grow and learn more.*

*I feel excited about this assignment, and I will work hard to make you proud!*

### Arrogant Language

*I am the one you want for this—no one can do it better than I can. I am sure of it.*

*Why would you pick him for the job? I am so much better than anyone here when it comes to that kind of work.*

*Thanks, but I don't need your suggestions. I know what I am doing here.*

*Nah, this isn't hard at all. I will do it perfectly—just wait and see!*

*You were smart to pick me for this. I am the best there is!*

When choosing your words, be mindful that children may interpret what you say differently than you intend even when you are speaking quite clearly. Two months after my boys arrived here from South Africa, I went on the road to do several speaking engagements. It was a hot, long August, and despite the fact that I enjoy doing speeches, I desperately wanted to be home with my new family. Every night when I called to speak to my husband and the boys, I told them how homesick I was and that I couldn't wait to see them.

Six days after my departure, Sisipho walked into the living room and asked Scotty if they could talk. Scotty nodded. Sisipho then said, "I am really worried about Mom. Whenever we talk to her, she says she is homesick. It has been six days, and she doesn't seem to be getting any better!"

Bless his heart.

The whole time, my precious son had been worried that I was at home (the hotel) and was truly sick. *Homesick* was just not a word he knew in South Africa.

We want to raise children with extensive vocabularies so that

> Always remember that words that uplift, support, connect, clarify, and instruct possess far more power than those that are used to impress.

they have the words they need to express their thoughts and ideas accurately; therefore, when relating to your students, be mindful of their vocabulary strengths and limitations. Introduce new words to students in meaningful ways and use new words when speaking to them. At the same time, be aware that, like my texts with Osei, too much is just too much. Most importantly, always remember that words that uplift, support, connect, clarify, and instruct possess far more power than those that are used to impress.

## CHAPTER SUMMARY

- Simple language often conveys your points more effectively.
- Your audience would rather understand your points than be impressed by your vocabulary.
- If you choose to use complex vocabulary, use it correctly!
- Confidence is attractive; arrogance is not.
- Language should be used to connect us, not confuse us.

## IMPLEMENTATION

If you are having difficulty relating to your audience, consider the words you chose to convey your message. Simple is often better. Seek the best words to get your point across in a meaningful way that develops rapport.

# Temptation

I t was time for my annual physical, and as the nurse took my blood pressure, we engaged in normal pleasantries.

"So, you are a teacher?" she asked.

"Yes, I teach middle school!" I smiled.

"Oh, I know you must be dreading heading back to work next week," she said.

"Well," I said, "I am actually really excited to start another year. I absolutely love what I do."

She dropped her clipboard and scurried out of the room. When you are having your blood pressure taken and the nurse runs away, it is never a good sign; consequently, I was fluctuating between confusion and panic by the time she returned.

As she entered, she pulled another nurse in by the sleeve and exclaimed, "Here she is! I told you there had to be one! I knew it!"

Perplexed, I said, "Excuse me?"

"I was just telling her that I knew there had to be one!"

"I'm sorry—I don't understand. One what?" I asked.

"One teacher who loves what she does! We have been seeing teachers all summer long, and you are the very first one to say that you love what you do. Every other one has complained and griped to the point that we both said that we plan to move by the time we have school-aged kids!"

The second nurse added, "She's right. We have been so depressed to know that there are so many teachers who actually hate going to school."

"Oh, no, I think you misunderstood them. You see, the reality is that teachers work really hard—the whole 'summer off' thing is a myth. Those who have complained about going back are just wishing for a little more time to be with family, get summer projects done, and do stuff like that. It doesn't mean they don't like teaching," I explained. "On another day, I might have said I needed more time before going back to school, too, even though I absolutely love being in the classroom."

If you are a teacher, you know that my explanation was completely valid. Despite my defense of my fellow educators, the nurses weren't buying it.

## COMPLAINING DOESN'T IMPROVE THINGS

Like all humans, I am tempted to complain. But when I am, I often think about those nurses. Even on the days when nothing is going right, we have reasons to be grateful. When my daughter Madison was a teenager and went through typical teen angst, I would say, "Tell me the one good thing about today." If you have a propensity to complain, ask yourself the same thing. If you start by focusing on what is good, you will be surprised how the good usually far outweighs the bad.

Social media can be a wonderful outlet for support if you are frustrated or overwhelmed, but be mindful how you post. Cryptic complaints are rarely cryptic. If you have an issue with work, think before you slam your organization for the whole world to see it. If someone has upset you, talk to the person directly.

**Attention-Seeking Post**

*I hate my life. I cannot do this another day if certain people do not step up and do their jobs and support me.*

**Appropriate Post for Support**

*I have had a challenging year as I adjust to my new position. Please keep me in your thoughts and prayers! If you have felt like I do and have some words of wisdom, please send them my way!*

**Attention-Seeking Post**

*How are you gonna do that to me and think you are gonna get away with it? You know who you are.*

**Appropriate Post**

(Don't post this publicly. Contact the person directly.) I *would love to talk with you about some issues that have weighed heavily upon my heart. Do you have time for a call or for a cup of coffee?*

Be mindful that once your words are out there, they are out there forever. Nothing is truly private. If you wouldn't want your boss, your coworkers, your students, your children, your family, your friends, or anyone else to see it, don't post it.

## GOSSIP POISONS RELATIONSHIPS

It is not only tempting to complain about circumstances; it is also tempting to talk about people. And this can be even more harmful. Did you ever witness mean girl drama as a teenager? I certainly did. In fact, one high school memory is still vividly etched in my mind even after all these years.

The routine was the same every day. Each morning I would see Jacinta in the hallway, and she would stop, smile, and hug me. "You look sooo pretty today!" she always said, as though on cue, with the same voice inflection and sing-songy cadence to her words. We would exchange pleasantries, and they were always oozing with compliments and kind words. Before we would depart to our homerooms, she would hug me again, squeeze my hand, and walk away. I craved her validation, but deep inside I knew that the exchanges were forced and fake.

Every few nights she would call me and tell me how wonderful I was and how glad she was to be my friend. On one such evening, her phone clicked while we were chatting. Someone was calling her. "Hold on, Kim. Someone is calling. Let me tell them I will call them back."

I heard a click, and then Jacinta's voice again. "Oh, my God! Guess who I am talking to? It is Kim. She drives me sooo crazy. She is always calling me and following me around. I am sooo tired of her copying me."

I felt like I had been punched in the gut. Tears immediately filled my eyes. I was frozen, unable to speak.

"Hello? Are you there? Let me call you back after I get rid of her."

"Hey," I finally said.

Silence. Then the line went dead. I can only assume she panicked and hung up after she realized that she had said everything to me instead of someone else.

*Ring . . . ring . . .* She tried to call again, but I turned off my ringer and cried myself to sleep. I was a junior in high school the night that happened, and I still remember how Jacinta made me feel small, insignificant, and manipulated. Since then, I have met many manipulators like Jacinta, and I am sure that you have, too. Now that I am wiser, I do not tolerate manipulation. My students will tell you that the one way to see my wrath is to be mean to someone else. I simply cannot and will not allow it.

But there are adults who are like Jacinta, too. Adults who manipulate, gossip, bully, and hurt those around them. Some adults never progress beyond that teenage mindset. And for some reason, we still crave their validation, just like I wanted Jacinta to be my friend even though I knew deep inside that she was not a good person.

I am not proud to admit it, but I, too, have given in to the temptation of gossiping in the past. But as I have grown wiser, I have realized that there is never a good time and place for it, and now I strive to avoid

**If your coworkers gossip *to* you, they also gossip *about* you when you aren't around.**

it at all costs. Why take pleasure in someone else's pain? Why use words to tear down instead of to build up? Also, be wary of those who gossip in your presence. After all, if your coworkers gossip *to* you, they also gossip *about* you when you aren't around. Don't get caught in that kind of a web.

Many years ago, I had a class of girls who were especially drawn to middle school drama. I loved these little girls fiercely, but I knew that I had to squash their constant whispering and gossiping; it was unhealthy and hurtful. I decided to find a way to rearrange the schedule so that I could meet alone with them.

I spoke to the girls about the power of their words and shared how people who talk about others usually do so because either they are insecure or jealous. The girls opened up and admitted that they had been unkind, even cruel to one another because of petty jealousies. There were many tears as they apologized to one another. But I wanted this conversation to be one they wouldn't soon forget, so I came prepared with a way to illustrate my point.

I placed a clear plastic cup containing light vegetable oil at each girl's desk. I asked the girls to describe the qualities of the oil.

*It is smooth.*

*Watch how it flows!*

*Mine is really clear.*

*It is helpful and makes things run better.*

Next, I pulled out some red vinegar. I told the girls how their unkind words are like that vinegar, sour and acidic. As I spoke, I shook a few dots of it into their cups of oil. Then, I told them to gently shake their cups one time. The red dots multiplied. I said that every time they gossiped, it was like shaking that cup; their unkindness was multiplied exponentially. I told them to shake the cups again, and they gasped as one or two red dots quickly turned into dozens of them.

"What can we learn from this?" I asked.

"Don't be vinegar!" said Shaylene.

"Exactly!" I replied.

And that was all that was needed. The girls kept each other in check for the rest of the year. Whenever a girl started to gossip, one of her classmates would inevitably say, "Don't be vinegar!" and that was that.

Adults can be just as guilty of that same type of gossip, and the effects can be just as detrimental and hurtful. What do you do if someone is speaking unkindly behind your back? Even so-called friends like Jacinta can turn on us with their words. If that happens to you, first try to find out the source of that person's complaint against you. Use the six principles to have a meaningful conversation with him or her. But if the person doesn't stop with the gossip, separate yourself. Who needs friends like that?

## SET THE EXAMPLE

In the workplace, separation isn't always an alternative. In any organization, people will vent and commiserate, but if you find that you are always behind closed doors whispering your complaints about someone or something, you are making your environment toxic. And others see you and know to be cautious around you. They may gossip with you, laugh along with you, or agree with what you say, but they won't trust you or respect you. Life is too short to be focused

> Success and happiness are not limited, like slices of a pie. There is more than enough to go around.

on petty jealousies. Success and happiness are not limited, like slices of a pie. There is more than enough to go around. In fact, if you celebrate others' success, you will be more likely to find your own.

## BE THE EXAMPLE

One of the most phenomenal women I have ever known was a coworker of mine named Mona. I worked closely with Mona for nine years. In nine years, I never heard her gossip once. Not one single time. Whenever you left the room, you knew that the only reason Mona would speak your name would be if it was to say something kind or complimentary. Mona's beautiful spirit and exemplary character had a profound effect upon the climate and culture of our entire school because everyone loved and admired this woman so very much. Her goodness made us all want to be better; everyone wanted to be like Mona. She radiated joy and kindness, and the ripple effect was immeasurable.

You must exude that which you hope to create. If you want to work in a place where coworkers positively seek solutions for challenges instead of complain about them, you must model that. If you want to be in an environment where others uplift, support, and care for others, you must demonstrate those behaviors.

> If you want to be in an environment where others uplift, support, and care for others, you must demonstrate those behaviors.

If you are a leader, it is pretty much guaranteed that at some point, your employees will talk about you or a decision that you did or did not make. In some cases, you just have to let it go and know that it comes with the territory; however, if one toxic employee is continually gossiping and spreading negativity, your best course of action is to confront that person. Here's what that might sound like:

> *I appreciate you taking the time to meet with me. I wanted to talk with you because I get the impression that you are not happy with the way I have handled some things, and I want to give you the opportunity to share your thoughts.*

> *Can we talk? My intuition is telling me that perhaps you have negative feelings toward me, and I would love to have the opportunity to clear things up.*

In some cases, this will lead to a wonderful dialogue if you follow the six principles. In other cases, the employee will deny everything and act like you are his or her favorite person on the planet, but at least you have let the employee know that you are aware of what they are doing. This usually dissuades the person from gossiping so much in the future.

Let your words be used to solve problems, offer suggestions, and help others. Use your speech to edify, uplift, and support. Be a driving force that inspires kindness.

## CHAPTER SUMMARY

- Those who complain or gossip are toxic to an organization.

- When posting social media, do not be cryptic or attention seeking.

- You must exude that which you hope to create.

- If someone is gossiping about you, ask to meet with them and gently confront them using the six principles.

## IMPLEMENTATION

The next time you find yourself gossiping, complaining, or spreading negativity, check yourself and change the dialogue. Remember when your mama said, "If you can't say anything nice, don't say anything at all?" This is sage advice. Use your words to find solutions or to edify others.

# Concentration

"**Y**ou will have sixty minutes to complete the clues, solve the puzzles, and Escape the Room! Your time begins now!" The door shut, and we heard the click of the lock.

Our staff, ever competitive, launched into overdrive as we began to turn the small space upside down. At first glance, there was very little to be found—a bookcase, desk, coatrack, table, dresser, and chair. I immediately began to look for a way to organize the books on the bookshelf to find some type of hidden message; Camille Jones began to seek connections among all of the clocks on the wall. Junior Bernadin found a map under the chair, and using the marked longitude and latitude, he unlocked a box inside the desk. "We've got the first clue!" he exclaimed.

As we worked independently and in tandem, there were many screams, shrieks, and laughs; however, we didn't waste a second unlocking the clues. The whole while, the clock on the screen ticked away. The time seemed to pass faster and faster as our anxiety grew. Hope King found a cape on a coatrack; Wade King figured out that if we held the cape over a picture on the wall, several letters appeared through holes that had been cut into it.

We began to find papers hidden in unlikely nooks and crannies, and we wove the clues together, piece by piece. When Camille unlocked another box, she found a cell phone—one that could be used to help with the final clue. The clock continued to count down until only moments remained. We panicked. On the floor, we had completed most of a puzzle: W __ T E __ L __ __.

"Waterloo! It's Waterloo!" I exclaimed. No one listened. Everyone clamored to find more codes, more clues to open the final lock. They flipped over seat cushions and searched for hidden compartments under desk drawers. Ben Walker began to disassemble the coatrack to see if it could be transformed into something else.

"Y'all, I really think it's Waterloo!" I shouted again. No one paid any attention.

Finally, Wade asked, "Waterloo? Why would . . . "

"TIME!" a booming voice yelled over the intercom.

My highly accomplished and even more competitive staff did not Escape the Room.

The final clue? Waterloo. The final lock code was 1815, the year of the Battle of Waterloo. We would have been allowed to search for the year on the cell phone.

And since that day, whenever my staff isn't listening, I yell, "Waterloo!" and they get the point. We have laughed and laughed about that night many times, but at the end of the day, the problem was that somewhere in the middle of the challenge, we forgot to concentrate on anyone but ourselves. We lost sight of the fact that we were stronger together. If we had listened to each other, we could have won the game and escaped.

Now, although I was the one who was not listened to while we were trying to escape the room, I have also been on the other side of the fence and have been the one who failed to do the listening. About two years ago, my husband and my children all told me I needed to get my hearing checked. Now that I am in my fifties and my vision has gone, I figured that my hearing must be next.

I set up an appointment for an extensive hearing test. I was placed in a sound-proof room and given headphones. Throughout the test, I had to listen for sounds at all different frequencies and note which ear could hear them. At the end of the test, the nurse sat down with me for my consultation.

"So, how bad is it?" I said. "Do I have to get a hearing aid?"

"Mrs. Bearden, your hearing is fine. In fact, you scored higher than I did on the test. Perhaps you have a lot on your mind since you are running a school and raising several kids of your own. Could that be it?"

That was her nice way of saying that I have selective hearing.

So believe me, I am not pointing fingers. I am a work in progress. Here are some simple changes that I have made, and I have noticed that they have made me a better listener, which makes me a better communicator. They have also helped me implement the six principles at a deeper level.

- When someone speaks to me, I put down the phone or turn my computer screen away from me. (I used to keep typing or texting away because I thought that I was a good multitasker.)

- When someone speaks to me and I am in the middle of something and didn't hear it, I say, "I am so sorry. I was concentrating on my text, but I really want to hear what you said. Can you please repeat it?" or, "What you said is important to me, but I didn't hear it. I am so sorry. Give me one second so that I can give you my undivided attention."

- When someone talks to me, I concentrate on being present—fully present.

I am still working to improve in this area, and I know that I am not alone in my challenge to concentrate on the here and now. As a society, we are so busy posting, texting, snapping, and tweeting that we often miss experiencing life's most beautiful moments because we are watching them through a cell phone lens rather than just seeing them through our own eyes. I want to preserve moments, but I also want to *live* moments. The balance can be difficult.

> I want to preserve moments, but I also want to *live* moments.

## TALK TO ME

When a student asks a question, stop, look, and listen. When students feel seen, they feel valued. When an adult speaks to you, do the same whether it be a coworker or a stranger. You validate their worth when you do so.

# CULTURE KILLERS

I have the opportunity to work with educators all over the country, and a lack of acknowledgement is one of the biggest factors that kills school culture and communication. Educators often share their biggest frustrations with me, and here are their most often expressed barriers to relationship building among their staff members:

- Failure to speak to one another in hallways

- Failure to smile

- Failure to support one another's success

- Failure to offer help to one another

- Failure to encourage and uplift one another

Administrators, here are culture killers that frustrate teachers. Some of your list is the same, but there are a few additional factors to consider:

- Failure to speak to one another in hallways

- Failure to smile

- Failure to support one another's success

- Failure to offer help to one another

- Failure to encourage and uplift one another

- Failure to acknowledge staff publicly

- Failure to communicate quickly after a formal observation

- Failure to give credit where it is due

- Failure to admit when you don't know the answer

- Failure to listen first

- Failure to show interest in your faculty members' lives

Here is the good news: All of these things are so easy to correct. But just because they are easy, do not discount their importance. If you are a school leader and you do not speak to your staff members in the hallway, paranoia can ensue. Here is what goes through some teachers' minds:

*Oh, my gosh. I knew he didn't like me.*

*Is he upset with me for some reason?*

*Did she not like my lesson?*

*Is she thinking about putting me on the transfer list?*

*Did she think that problem was my fault?*

Teachers have so much on their plates, and when you fail to validate and acknowledge them, it can lead them into a spiral of negative thinking. Stop, speak, smile, look, listen. Most importantly, concentrate on living in the moment because once a moment has passed, you can never experience it again.

## CHAPTER SUMMARY

- We are stronger together than when we try to function independently without listening to one another.

- When we interact with others, we need to take the time to stop, look, listen, and concentrate.

- A failure to acknowledge others can be a huge roadblock to communication in your organization.

## IMPLEMENTATION

Be mindful of your attention level when interacting with others. Do you need to put the phone down? Close the computer? Stop writing? Make a concerted effort to concentrate more on the people around you and to live in the moment.

## chapter 15

# Location

I hadn't spoken to Nita in several months, so when her name showed up on my caller ID at 3:00 a.m., I knew I'd better answer.

"Nita, is that you? What's going on?"

"Um, Mrs. Bearden, I'm kind of in a situation. I'm sorry I woke you up. I didn't know who else to call."

"Are you okay?" I asked.

"I think so," she answered.

Now fully awake, I felt the anxiety rising in my throat. "Where are you?"

"I'm not sure. Well, I am in a parking lot, but I don't know the exact address. I am somewhere in South Carolina, though, and, um, I think I need help."

"Okay. I am here. Are you safe in that parking lot? Is there somewhere elsewhere you can go? Are you hurt? Tell me everything!" I implored.

She responded, "Well, remember that guy I was dating? Well, I went home from school with him during our semester break. We are now staying at his brother's apartment. We started to argue, and he threatened to hurt me. He raised his hand at me like he was about to hit me, and the look in his eyes really scared me. I ran from the apartment, and now I don't know exactly what to do. I don't have any money with me, and I don't have a car. I don't even know exactly where I am.

I just can't go back into that apartment. I am afraid he will be even angrier now because I left." The catch in her voice told me she was trying to hold in the tears.

"Okay, it is going to be all right. I will take care of you, honey. Just listen very carefully and do as I say."

I calmly reminded Nita how to find her location on her phone. Keeping her on the line, I grabbed my husband's phone and booked a hotel nearby. I gave her my credit card to put into her Uber app, and told her to stay on the line with me until she arrived safely at the hotel. Once she was safe and sound, I told her to go to sleep, and in the morning, I would call her with her flight information; I would use my Sky Miles to fly her home.

When I picked her up from the airport that afternoon, she hugged me so tightly that it took my breath away. Weary, she fell asleep on the way back to my house. I tucked her in on my couch and let her sleep some more. When she awakened, we talked about her situation and came up with her plan so that she could completely remove herself from the relationship.

Midsentence, she stopped and thanked me again. "Mrs. Bearden, I am so grateful you answered that phone. When we were just little girls in your class, you told us that you would always be there for us. Lots of people say that, but I knew you meant it. It has been years since then, and yet when I needed you the most, you showed up."

I cried from the exhaustion and relief of it all, but I also cried because I was grateful that I had answered that call. My bed had been so warm and cozy, and when I had heard the phone ring, I wanted to turn it off and roll over. But I had promised that I would always be there for Nita, and I needed to be good at my word.

Nita's story is a reminder that we need to say what we mean and mean what we say. Ron and I have a policy at our school: Never ever make a promise to a child unless you

> Never ever make a promise to a child unless you plan to keep it.

plan to keep it. Don't tell kids you are going to go somewhere, do something, or experience something unless you are 100 percent sure you will be able to make good on that promise. Don't tell a child you are going to watch his baseball game or meet him for lunch if you can't be sure it will happen. Sometimes things come up, but you have to follow up and follow through.

One of my precious students, Navaeh, shares a birthday with me. In September, we talked about sharing a celebratory lunch together, but her schedule is almost as busy as mine, and we couldn't find a single Saturday to make it happen. Navaeh said, "It's okay, Mrs. Bearden. I know things are busy right now!" But I was determined to follow through because I had given my word. Numerous times I told Navaeh that we would have our lunch over our next break instead, and we did just that. It was a lovely time. When I dropped her off at her house, Navaeh said, "Thank you for really making it happen, Mrs. Bearden! I had so much fun!"

Too many children have experienced too many broken promises already, and when we fail to follow through on our promises, we add to the cycle of heartache and mistrust. Even those children who live in supportive environments need to see us model honesty and integrity if we hope to help build those traits in them.

## THE DISHONESTY TRAP

Honesty isn't only important when dealing with children. If you weave a web of lies, it will eventually catch up with you. People lie for many reasons, but both children and adults will sometimes lie to cover for themselves. I love my team and the honest stream of communication we share. We are all juggling multiple roles, and so when one of us messes up—and we all do—we acknowledge it. "That was my mistake—I take complete responsibility. I apologize, and it won't happen again." And we all move on—no harm, no foul. Think about it: When individuals in your organization try to cover up, make excuses, or deflect blame, you lose respect for them. But if someone says, "Okay, I admit it. I ate that pie in the refrigerator; I didn't realize you were saving it for your class. I feel terrible and I am sorry," you respect them for confessing and move on.

People sometimes lie to promote themselves, usually in hopes of receiving validation. If you find yourself lying to make yourself look better, consider why you feel the need to do so. Do you want people to respect you for who you really are, or for a false projection of who you are?

Finally, people lie to promote their own agendas. Many years ago, we had a mother whom I will call Ms. Busybody. No matter how much we did for her or her child, she would find fault. Complaining like that used to break my heart, but Ron helped me understand. "Kim, don't let it hurt you. You could give everyone a Porsche, and somebody would complain that it isn't red." I have now learned to consider that there are some individuals who project their own unhappiness unto everyone else, no matter how much you try to appease them. Ms. Busybody's constant pot stirring was relentless, and it wreaked havoc and misunderstanding among some of our parents.

She sent Ron and me an email:

*I am writing on behalf of all of the parents. They are upset because we haven't received our school photos yet. I just wanted to let you know what they are saying because I know you would want to know that they are extremely dissatisfied with how long it has taken. When can I tell them that the pictures will be distributed?*

I have pretty wonderful parents, and although I am sure that they did want those photos, I highly doubted that they would be in an uproar about it. Ron doubted it too, so he asked Ms. Busybody to come in for a conference with us.

"Ms. Busybody, thank you for coming in to meet with us. We know you are really busy. We appreciate you sending us an email—we have always said that we want to know if our parents are upset, and it sounds like they are!" I said.

Ms. Busybody nodded and shifted in her seat.

"Ms. Busybody, this is troublesome to us that so many parents are upset," Ron said. "When you said you were emailing on behalf of all of the parents, whom were you referring to?"

"All of them. All of the parents in our class, of course," she replied.

"Oh, goodness!" Ron answered. "I guess I should meet with them all if they are so unhappy. I am unsure if I should have a class meeting or just meet with the ones who are the unhappiest. Can you tell me the names of those who have really expressed dissatisfaction?" he asked.

"Well, it is just everyone. But I will tell them what we talked about. You don't have to meet with them," she said.

Ron continued, "If this truly is a problem and they feel like we are nonresponsive, I want to meet with them all. Let's see—let me go down the list of parents' names, and you can tell me whom you think I need to talk to first."

I watched as Ms. Busybody cleared her throat and started rummaging through her purse to find a cough drop.

As Ron asked each name, she shook her head. Finally, Ron said, "Ms. Busybody, did anyone specifically tell you they were upset, or did you just make that assumption?"

"I know that all the mothers have to be upset about those pictures, so I just spoke on their behalf."

"Did they ask you do speak on their behalf?" I asked.

"Well, no. But I was just trying to be helpful," she said.

*Sigh.* The whole thing was a lie to push her personal agenda. I felt sad for Ms. Busybody. What she really longed for was respect from the fellow parents. She wanted to be a leader and to be admired for speaking out; she desperately wanted to be the class spokesperson. Because of the lies she wove, she ended up embarrassed and tangled in a web of deceit.

Your word is important. If you want to be a leader who uplifts and inspires, be truthful. Admit when you don't know the answer; admit when you are wrong. And if you are going to say you will be there, by goodness, keep your word and be there.

## CHAPTER SUMMARY

- When you tell someone that you will be there for them, you must keep your word.

- If you make a promise, be sure that you can follow through on it.

- People lie to protect themselves, promote themselves, or push their agendas. Recognize this and do not fall into the same trap.

- Those who model honesty and integrity help to promote those traits in their organizations.

## IMPLEMENTATION

Reflect upon your words, and when you are tempted to be untruthful, ask yourself why you feel led to be dishonest. Adjust your course and speak honestly. Choose your words carefully so that when others think of you, they know that they can count on you to be there.

## chapter 16

# Adoration

I t was going to be a special Halloween. Fifteen of our students had been invited to perform at a conference in Orlando, and we were thrilled when we were gifted with tickets to Universal Studios. Like most school groups, our students always wear matching T-shirts on field trips; however, Ron had a clever idea up his sleeve.

"Kim, let's get fake T-shirts for our kids that will be their Halloween costumes!" he said, his eyes alight with a look I had learned to recognize as Ron's own form of creative mischief.

I played along. "Fake T-shirts? Sounds perfect! But what on earth do you mean?"

"Well," he replied, "instead of putting 'The Ron Clark Academy' on them, let's put the name of a made-up school. Something that will arouse curiosity. I was thinking they should say 'The Hollywood School for Children of Celebrities.'"

I thought his idea was genius, so we found a random crest online, created a simple design, and placed our order. When the students saw the finished products, they could not stop laughing. "People will think we are really important! Oh, my gosh—what will they do?"

Our day was an intriguing social experiment to say the least. This was at a time when cell phone cameras had just become common, and we watched as people tried to snap our students' pictures without us noticing. Many pointed; others followed us at a close distance.

Wherever we went, our students were treated as celebrities themselves. I was tickled by the way that they assumed their roles with great finesse. They fell into character and carried themselves with a definite swagger and confidence. After following us for a good ten minutes, a middle-aged woman in a Def Leppard T-shirt and a mullet walked up to the group and said, "Who are your parents? I have to know! Please tell me. I can't take the guessing anymore!"

One of our more dramatic eighth graders, Kennedy, responded, "Ma'am, I am so sorry, but I am sure that you can understand that because of security concerns, we are not permitted to disclose that information."

I swallowed a huge giggle; we all did.

The woman was not happy with this response. "Then why on earth wear those shirts? It just torments us! Well, can I at least get a picture with all of you?"

We happily obliged.

Please don't send me letters telling me that we shouldn't encourage our students to lie. We don't. This was just a harmless Halloween joke; however, that day was a memorable adventure, and the lessons learned were valuable despite the hilarity of it all. Whenever we take students on a trip, we always end the night with circle time, an opportunity for students to reflect upon their experiences. That evening, my students' comments were both comical and insightful.

"We were made to feel so special!"

"Wow! I wish I was always treated like that!"

"Everyone admired us so much!"

And then, "They just treated us that way because of who they thought our parents are. Shouldn't everyone be treated special? And even if our parents were celebrities, it doesn't mean that they were necessarily nice people or better than anyone else."

"You're right," I said. "Everyone should be treated well. We should want to get to know someone for who they are, not because of their fame or fortune."

## VALUE THE WORTH OF ALL PEOPLE

All people have value, all have worth. Yet in our world, we often fail to show adoration to people for their humanity, their kindness, or their goodness; instead, we adore those who have perceived prestige or importance. As for me, I choose to surround myself with people who adore other human beings for who they are, not their social status.

Are you thinking about hiring someone? Here's a tip: Take the applicant to a restaurant and watch how he or she treats the waiter. If the applicant is rude, dismissive, or difficult, do not offer the position. Trust me! People who are rude to service workers are not only rude to service workers; their behavior bleeds into their other professional interactions as well. Ron and I have chosen not to hire several candidates because of the way that they treated a service professional, one of our security guards, or members of our staff. (If you are looking to be hired somewhere, treat everyone in that building with respect; every interaction is an interview of sorts!) Ron and I also both have a theory that everyone should wait tables at some point in life—we both have. If you do, you will forever treat service professionals with respect.

> People who are rude to service workers are not only rude to service workers; their behavior bleeds into their other professional interactions as well.

But my point goes beyond simple courtesy. Preconceived ideas about certain groups of people—prejudices—influence your communication style and interactions. Do you speak to the lady who cleans your hotel room or the restrooms at your workplace, or do you act like she is invisible and walk on by? Do you introduce yourself to your tour bus driver? What about the employee at the gas station where you go several times a week? Do you look your cashier in the eyes when you say "thank you," or are you dismissive in your interactions? Do you know the names of your lunchroom workers? If your server has multiple face piercings and a tattooed, shaved head, do you engage differently than if the server looks more like you? If so, seek to see the heart of the person, not the exterior. And even if the person doesn't respond as you would like—perhaps his or her heart has hardened—then you have still shown unconditional love, and that is a beautiful thing.

My precious daughter, Madison, has never met a stranger. She is outgoing and bold, small yet mighty. She is a successful hair stylist and owns her own studio. While she is very talented at doing hair, I believe that it is her ability to connect with people from every walk of life that makes her so successful. Her clients represent incredibly varied backgrounds. From suburban housewife soccer moms to tattooed, purple-haired exotic dancers, she connects with them all. They open up to her and share their heartaches and triumphs.

On more than one occasion, I have heard her tell a client, "Oh, my gosh! Tell me *everything*!" And they do.

Recently we were talking about this, and Madison laughed and said, "Mim, they really do tell me unbelievable things!"

"Like what?" I probed.

"Mim, you know I can't tell you. They trust me—they tell me because they know that I won't say anything, even to my mother!"

I love that my daughter actually uses the six principles in her daily interactions, and this has enabled her to empower others while doing what she loves.

## DIVINE APPOINTMENTS

Like everyone else, there are times when I just don't feel like being social. But I do believe that our days are filled with divine appointments—moments where we have the opportunity to communicate with others in a way that uplifts them, validates them, or even soothes their soul. At other times, such encounters provide us with the opportunity to be the recipient of such blessings.

On a warm spring afternoon, I was anxiously running errands, trying to get everything done in a short time span. I had more to accomplish than there were hours in the day. (We teachers have to take care of everything on the weekends since we live at school all week long!) I had been putting off getting my car cleaned, but I couldn't stand it any longer. As I pulled into the line at the carwash, I sighed. I knew this task would take more time than I wanted to spend, but I felt like it had to be done for my sanity. I grabbed my phone and trudged into the waiting area, determined to find a quiet corner alone where I could answer my emails and make the best use of my time.

I found just the spot—an isolated, comfy bench right near the window. As soon as I settled in, she sat right beside me: an elderly woman who was humming incessantly. I barely looked up, acknowledged her with a smile, and went back to work, wishing I had some earphones. She had other plans, though, and they included engaging me in conversation. To be honest, I just wanted to be left alone. But I could tell that she was not going to give up easily, and so I put the phone down and truly looked at her for the first time.

She was stunning, even radiant. I learned that she was eighty-two years old, and her name was Fran. She was humming because she was studying a book of piano music. As she hummed the melodies, she moved her gnarled, spotted hands across her lap, as if she were playing an imaginary keyboard.

With sparkling eyes, Fran shared that she had just started taking piano lessons and that she was so excited to play music for the first time in her life. I told her that I used to play, but I never seemed to find the time to do so anymore. I was deeply touched by this precious woman's passion for her newfound hobby, and I told her that she inspired me.

Fran went on to tell me that her husband, Bill, who had been blind for eleven years, was the real inspiration. They had been married for sixty-two years, and he still took care of their farm and drove his tractor every day, despite his blindness. She giggled and shared that he had recently started learning German at age eighty-three, just because he always wanted to speak another language. Her face emanated pure devotion as she spoke of her beloved life partner.

We chatted for a while, and when the receptionist announced that my car was finished, I couldn't believe that it was already time to go. As I rose to leave, Fran took my hand and said, "Dear, go home and play your piano. If there is something you want to learn, study it. If there is something you want to make, create it. God gives us gifts, and it is our job to use them with all that we are. Cherish every moment of your life."

Her warmth flowed through me. Perhaps I was entertaining an angel unaware. Thank you, sweet Fran, for blessing me and teaching me that when we take the time to notice and to engage with others (even a stranger we may never see again), we may experience some of life's most beautiful moments. Moments worthy of adoration.

## CHAPTER SUMMARY

- All people should be treated with respect, regardless of social status or differences.

- When we engage with others in our day-to-day lives, we should take the time to speak to them, look them in the eyes, and validate them.

- Our days are filled with divine appointments—opportunities to interact with others and uplift them. Doing so uplifts us as well.

## IMPLEMENTATION

As you go through your daily routine, take note of how often you engage with the people you encounter. Make a conscious effort to say "thank you," look people in the eyes, and acknowledge their worth no matter who they are.

## chapter 17

# Illumination

always loved school—the crackle of textbooks, the feel of my pen gliding across the page, and the thrill of discovering new ideas empowered me. I always knew that school would be where I would choose to spend the rest of my life. I knew deep in my soul that I wanted to change the world; I wanted to live a life with purpose. So as I prepared to graduate from the University of Georgia, I set my sights on finding my first teaching position—hopefully one where I could reach children who needed me.

It was a beautiful March day in the spring of 1987 when I had my first teaching interview. I felt confident and accomplished. My portfolio contained glowing evaluations, and my grades were exemplary. My professors had assured me that any school would be thrilled to have an enthusiastic young teacher like me. I put on my best drop-waisted floral dress, gathered my 80s-permed hair into a large red bow, and placed my crisp résumé into my new leather binder.

As I strode across the commons area of the job fair to table number six, I saw him waiting for me. The tall, dark-skinned black man in a navy suit watched me bebop toward him. He did not smile. At all. I became self-conscious and then nervous, and then completely flustered. As he stood, I awkwardly shook his hand, and he gestured for me to take a seat. He politely grilled me with questions, and I started to relax and regain my composure as my answers started to flow. And then he leaned in, smiled, and said, "Can you tell me what on earth you know about teaching black children?"

I stuttered, I stammered, I rambled on about loving children and wanting to make a difference. I shared lessons I had created that would be engaging. I talked about my passion for learning. I never actually answered his question, though. In fact, I even stumbled when I tried to say "black children," like that was something to be whispered. Like it was wrong to point out that yes, some children are black, and I am white. *Wouldn't that be impolite?* I thought. Sweat trickled down the back of my neck. He nodded and listened intently. The more I squirmed, the more stoically he sat. Finally, he released me from my misery and said, "Thank you, Miss Driscoll. I wish you the best."

I ran-walked out across the commons, holding my breath until I was able to make it to a corridor where tears sprung forth and spilled down my cheeks. I was confused. I was embarrassed. I was hurt, and then I became angry. *How dare he judge me? He hates me just because I am white. He is racist! I don't want that job anyway!* I thought. *I love all children, and that is enough! I will show him!*

It took me years to realize this difficult truth: He was right. I didn't know a thing.

Yes, I loved, supported, challenged, and uplifted countless students of color early in my career. And I taught them well; however, the very best teachers of all are able to connect to their students on multiple levels—they are able to draw connections between what students know and what they need to know. Master teachers are able to make learning relevant to students' life experiences; therefore, although I wholeheartedly poured myself into teaching and loving my kids, the depth of my ability to understand them and see the world through their lens was completely shortsighted. My shortsightedness and lack of awareness of race and culture was most likely passed on to the predominately white classes of students whom I taught, too. How could I truly see the world through the eyes of my black students when I even stumbled over saying that they were black in the first place?

# Illumination

As I evolved as a more culturally aware teacher, I started to notice the lack of diversity in the materials we used to teach. I noticed the absence of notable black authors, the omission of brown faces in textbooks and on novel covers, the failure to mention great blacks in history, save Rosa Parks and MLK during the obligatory Black History Month lessons in February. Even with this realization, it still took until I had the opportunity to work with teachers who could better educate me that I realized just how vast the cultural desert is in our schools even today. I am so grateful for the teachers at the Ron Clark Academy like Susan Barnes, Pamela Haskins, Camille Jones, Ben Walker, and Junior Bernadin who have lovingly enlightened and guided me. Most importantly, I am grateful for how they have poured into our students and visiting educators, sharing a wealth of knowledge about race and culture and how it affects our students' lives each and every day.

Here is another truth that I don't like to admit: If my memory is correct, my interview on that day was my first real conversation that I had ever had with a black man. Ever. In twenty-one years. I had spent my childhood in predominately white neighborhoods and schools. I had been raised to love all people and to be kind to people—and I modeled that—but I had never sat down with anyone of color and had a real, heart-to-heart conversation about anything. My interactions had all been casual, polite banter that occurred when encountering others in day-to-day life. Why had I been scared when I had seen him staring at me? Would I have been as scared if he had been white? I would like to tell you that I absolutely would have reacted in the same way. But I am not so sure. We fear what we do not know. I did not ever take the time to know anyone who was black. I didn't fear that he would hurt me, but I did fear that he would hate me and not understand me because I was a white sorority girl with a big red bow. That is something to think about, isn't it? I wonder how many times a day my black brothers and sisters feel the fear of being misjudged. Probably more than I will ever be able to adequately comprehend.

The twenty-one-year-old version of me could never have imagined that one day, I would be the mother to three beautiful black African sons. I never could have imagined that I would be on another side of the lens, horrified and heartbroken that someone could fear my precious, kind, loving boys without any reason beyond the color of their skin.

I certainly do not speak for all white people, and obviously others' experiences can differ greatly from mine. But I can say with certainty that there are many out there like me—white people who were raised to love, respect, and care for all races, but who never truly sought to understand the black experience. But ignorance is not an excuse; ignorance is the problem.

> Ignorance is not an excuse; ignorance is the problem.

Some of my white brothers and sisters who were also raised to love all people are also the same ones who can feel extremely defensive about discussions surrounding race because, "Hey, I am not a racist! I love all people. I have black friends! I am so tired of hearing about race. Why can't people just get over it and move on? Slavery is over, and I had nothing to do with it!" Some of them may choose to skip over the words in this chapter.

## THE NEED TO SEEK UNDERSTANDING

Herein lies the sorrow—the mistaken belief that life is the same for all of us. It is often believed that the world provides us all with the same conveniences that we are able to navigate with the same degree of ease. But underneath it all—the laws for equality, the opportunities for advancement, and even the pleasantries among us, there is a deeper layer—a layer that often manifests itself as fear, anger, confusion, hatred, impatience, irritation, or even indifference. It is this layer that seeps into our hearts like poison and seeks to destroy our humanity. If we don't recognize it, acknowledge it, and learn to talk about it, the wedge among us will grow greater and stronger, and hatred will win.

I have grown to realize that unless someone else has walked in your shoes, they will never completely understand what it feels like to be you. Your pain, your frustrations, and your suffering are exclusively unique to you. One can speculate, one can empathize, but there are certain realities one can never know without sharing the same life experiences.

Think about a time in your own life where you felt completely misunderstood. Some of us shut down in these circumstances and build up walls; we isolate ourselves as a means of self-preservation. Others of us act out in anger and frustration. Still others grow depressed, sad, and unable to function. Have you ever responded in this way? I know I have.

Have you had a situation where you felt like no one was listening despite your efforts to explain? Did you finally decide it was easier just to say nothing? Yep, I have done that, too.

Have you felt like others have dismissed your frustrations and implied that you were just being overly sensitive? Did their lack of understanding add to your frustrations? Check.

Have you grown angry, only to have someone tell you that you are being too dramatic? When they told you to calm down, did it make you even angrier? Yes.

Have you ever tried to explain your circumstances, only to have someone else tell you all of their own problems and how much worse they have it? Did this make you feel like they were minimizing your own challenges and making it about them instead? Many times.

If you have never experienced one of these scenarios, then you have had the rare privilege of being surrounded by people who completely get you all the time. Most of us aren't so lucky. We all experience being misunderstood. Just think back to the angst of your teenage years, and surely you will remember the feeling that others don't have any idea what it is like to be you.

My faith has taught me to love all people—I believe that love is our most powerful weapon against hatred. Love conquers all. But here is the great truth that has illuminated my perspective: When someone loves me, I also want and need that person to *understand* me. Don't you want the same? Most of us have had those arguments with our loved ones that go something like this: "I know you love me, but that is not the point! How can you not understand where I am coming from on this? How can you see this so differently than I do? I don't feel like you are listening at all!"

These are the conversations and frustrations we have with those who have walked similar paths; therefore, the difficulty of understanding others who have lived a completely different reality is so much greater. And of course, I am not only talking about black and white differences—I am talking about every kind of diversity.

Imagine a world where we could all be intentional about developing relationships with those who are different than we are. This doesn't mean that you would have to change your faith, your belief system, your values, morals, or political party. Imagine a world where we could approach each other in love and say, "I don't understand, but I care about you and I want to understand. Can you help me see this from your perspective?" Imagine if we all prayed not only for love but also for insight.

> Imagine if we all prayed not only for love but also for insight.

If your soul truly aches for this world, then consider being intentional about developing relationships with those who have seen the world through a different lens. Start the conversation. Start from a place of love and then listen more than you speak. You can even agree to disagree, but relentlessly continue to pursue perspective. If we could all seek understanding, we truly could change the world.

## CHAPTER SUMMARY

- There is a difference between truly knowing someone and just knowing of them.

- Our own life experiences shape our insight and understanding of those who have experienced life through a different lens.

- When you love someone, they don't only want you to love them; they also want you to understand them.

- We should seek out relationships with those who have seen the world through a different lens.

## IMPLEMENTATION

Reflect on your life experiences and how they shaped your perspectives and views of those who are different than you. Are there areas where you lack understanding? If so, seek insight. Start the conversation from a place of love. If you have a friend of a different race, and you have never talked about race with one other, make it happen. If you do not have access to people who are from different backgrounds than you are because of where you live, then seek perspective by reading articles, blogs, essays, and books by those who have walked a different path. Keep an open heart and mind as you read.

# Transformation

S he always had a big heart, but it could easily be shattered. She was filled with faith, hope, and love, but she was fueled by accomplishments, acceptance, and ambition. She pushed herself to achieve, but others had the power to dictate her emotions and control her joy. She cared about people and wanted to help them, but her good intentions had limitations that she didn't even know existed; her lack of understanding created barriers to her wisdom. She wanted to make the world better, but she wanted to avoid pain, struggle, or conflict while working toward her goals. She wanted to be with other people, to engage with them and laugh with them and enjoy them, but more than anything, she wanted them to make her feel whole.

Sometimes she changed who she was to morph into what she thought they wanted her to be. Sometimes she said she agreed with what they said, simply because she wanted them to like her. She projected perfectionism, but she often felt small and insecure. When her whole world fell apart, she sought meaning and realized that perhaps she had really needed to lose herself to find herself. And when she finally understood, she was transformed.

**How do I know these things? I am she.**

I have often wished that I could go back to the twenty-something version of myself and teach her the principles I have shared with you. I'd like to think that I would have listened, but now I am grateful that I had to discover them the hard way. Deep inside, I know that it was in times of darkness that I became the most enlightened; it was in my weakness that I became strong.

I am still highly competitive, ambitious, driven, and determined. But when I go to meet my Heavenly Father, I want my heart to be filled, not my bank account. I want to know that my power came from empowering others. I want to be able to say that I found beauty in brokenness and that I sought significance over achievements. I want to know that my happiness came from spreading joy to others and that I fought for what I believed in no matter how difficult the circumstances. I want to know that I didn't find my confidence in how others saw me; I found it through seeing the positive influence that I had upon others. I want to be able to say that I measured my success by how I lived my life for the world, not by how I lived it for myself. I want to know that I never stopped striving, seeking, listening, learning, and loving. When I am gone, I want there to be more laughter than tears because my life was one that was well used.

I have the same wishes for you, my friend. I hope that my words have planted seeds that will take root within you to help you produce your best life, a life where your relationships are enhanced and embraced, a life more magnificent than you can imagine.

Love and blessings,

# Part 3
# Situations and Simulations

You are now ready to put the six principles into practice, and the following exercises are designed to help you refine your skills.

# WRITTEN CORRESPONDENCE

In written correspondence, it is obvious that you are not engaging in the fifth principle, *conversation*, in a traditional sense; however, you are still engaging in discourse with a focus on a major component of the fifth principle: *information*. (Additional follow-up emails might be needed to seek *clarification* as well.) When providing *information* in written correspondence, it is important to be . . .

Concise

Clear

Humble

Friendly

Responsive

Grammatically correct

Open minded

Helpful. (Be sure to offer solutions and support.)

A repeat of *appreciation* and/or *validation* can serve as a means of *celebration* and the closing of your written correspondence:

*Thank you again for all that you do!*

*I appreciate you and your help with this.*

*I am grateful for your patience.*

*Thank you for being such a supportive parent.*

*I am grateful for your help. You are a blessing!*

*Thank you for raising such an incredible child.*

*Your child makes my day brighter, and I am so grateful to have the opportunity to teach him.*

The chart on the next page will help you see how all of these steps look when put together.

# THE 6 PRINCIPLES: Written Correspondence

## Internal Dialogue

### 1. Consideration
*What could be the other person's perspective?*

*Thoughts sound like...*

I wonder what could have triggered that email?

Something is obviously going on that I don't understand.

Is she going through some type of personal crisis?

Could we have done something else that upset her, and she is just responding to suppressed anger about it now?

If he is experiencing some type of problems, how can I let him know that we care?

I need to figure out how to fix this for the sake of everyone involved.

### 2. Motivation
*What do I want to be the outcome?*
*What should be driving me?*

| Positive Motivators | | Versus | Negative Motivators | |
|---|---|---|---|---|
| Compassion | Love | | Anger | Ignorance |
| Dedication | Patience | | Attention | Insecurity |
| Determination | Peace | | Control | Jealousy |
| Diligence | Persistence | | Defensiveness | Manipulation |
| Empathy | Positivity | | Ego | Negativity |
| Engagement | Productivity | | Fear | Power |
| Gentleness | Resolution | | Frustration | Revenge |
| Goodness | Service | | Greed | Selfishness |
| Grit | Significance | | Guilt | Sloth |
| Insight | Solutions | | Hatred | Suspicion |
| Joy | Truth | | | |
| Kindness | Wisdom | | | |

## External Dialogue

### 3. Appreciation
*What am I grateful for in this situation?*

*Sounds like...*

Thank you for taking the time to share your concerns with me...

I appreciate you setting up this time to talk so that we can find a solution...

I am grateful for your time. It means a lot to me...

It is helpful to hear what you are feeling. Thank you for telling me...

I am grateful that you trust me with your concerns...

I appreciate that you have been so open with me about your frustrations...

### 4. Validation
*How can I make the other person feel respected and heard?*

*Sounds like...*

I hope you are having a relaxing summer– you deserve it!

You did an amazing job. How did you come up with the inspiration to do it?

How do you handle all of this at once?

This was a huge task to accomplish. What made it the most difficult for you?

If it were a perfect world, what would you have changed about this situation?

Are you having a tough day? How can I help make it better for you?

### 5. Conversation
*Provide Information and Seek Clarification*

**Share your thoughts, ideas, or information that is...**

| | |
|---|---|
| Concise | Responsive |
| Clear | Grammatically correct |
| Humble | Open minded |
| Friendly | Helpful |

**Ask clarifying questions when needed.**
*Sounds like...*

Can you provide some more details about the situation?

### 6. Celebration
*Use Appreciation and Validation as your closing.*
*Sounds like...*

Thank you again for all that you do!

I appreciate you and your help with this.

I am grateful for your patience.

Thank you for being such a supportive parent.

I am grateful for your help– you are a blessing!

Thank you for raising such a respectful child.

Your child makes my day brighter, and I am so grateful to have the opportunity to teach him.

Here is a sample email exchange, showing this pattern. Remember: Internal dialogue consists of consideration and motivation, which guide the other four principles that are expressed in my response.

*Dear Teacher,*

*I would like to know why Jeremy received a detention last Thursday. He said that he was only saying, "God bless you" to the child sitting beside him. I feel like this is out of bounds and ridiculous. I would not sign his detention form. Thank you for correcting this error.*

*Sincerely,*
*Parent*


*Dear Parent,*

*Thank you for reaching out to me to clarify things—I appreciate you contacting me to get the details. Yes, Jeremy did say, "God bless you," but that is a good thing! He always does have good manners! The detention, however, was because he did not bring his iPad to class. I am not sure if he told you, but I require him to have it every day so that he can complete his tasks and participate. I did ask if there was a reason that he didn't have it, but he just responded with, "No, ma'am." Unfortunately, the detention still stands; however, I do appreciate Jeremy's honest and polite response. Thank you for understanding and for reaching out. I am grateful for you!*

*Sincerely,*
*Teacher*


On the pages that follow, you will find samples of emails for various situations. These are designed for practice, either independently or in group studies. After you have read each email, write your response before looking at the sample responses that I have provided. Use the chart on page 153 to help you. Keep in mind that my writing style might be very different from yours, but the examples should help with structure. The level of formality of your writing should match the level of formality of your relationship. Also, when addressing the recipient, always make sure that his/her name is correctly spelled. For simplification, I have used "Dear Parent," but please use the parent's name in real situations.

# FOR EDUCATORS

*Dear Teacher,*

*I am concerned about my daughter's grade on your project. She was up all night working on it, and I can't believe she received a 75 on it. Can you please tell me how you arrived at that grade? I am so frustrated!*

*Thank you,*
*Parent*

*Dear Parent,*

*Thank you for your email—it helps to know when something is heavy on your heart. I can understand your frustration, but please rest assured that this project is just one part of your daughter's grade, and she will have many opportunities to bring it up to her usual standard of excellence. There were many wonderful, clever parts of your daughter's project, and she truly has an artistic gift—Mrs. Barnes is going to love having her in her art class! There was a rubric that the students had to follow, however, and 60 percent of the grade was based on content. Unfortunately, this was where your daughter's grade suffered. I have attached the rubric in case she didn't show it to you before. If you would like for me to go over it with her to show her just how she received her deductions, I will be happy to do so after school.*

*Again, thank you for reaching out.*

*Best,*
*Teacher*

## TALK TO ME

*Dear Teacher,*

*I got my child's test scores back, and it looks like Billy did not grow at all from seventh to eighth grade. How can this be? I am worried that this will negatively impact his ability to get into a good high school. Please tell me what you plan to do to help him so that he will achieve at a higher rate.*

*Thank you.*
*Parent*


*Good evening, Parent!*

*I hope you have been doing well. I was actually going to reach out to you about that score because I knew it would worry you. I am so glad you beat me to it! I understand why you feel stressed—this high school stuff can be overwhelming. Let me try to put you at ease . . .*

*First of all, Billy's high school career is based on far more than the ITBS. This score reflects one hour on one day of the year, and your son is so much more than that! I am not sure what happened on the test, either, and I do not think that the score reflects Billy's true skill level. I have seen continued growth with your son throughout the year, and his grades are strong across the board. Fortunately, I will also have the opportunity to write your son's recommendation, and I will be sure to include details about his academic strengths and work ethic. I assure you that I will pay close attention to his progress in the areas where he didn't do as well on the test, and if I feel like there is an area where he is struggling, I will work with him one-on-one. If you see any cause for concern when he is doing his homework, don't hesitate to let me know.*

*Thank you for your support. You are an awesome dad!*

*Blessings,*
*Teacher*

*Dear Teacher,*

*My son Jake had a football game last night, and he was unable to complete his homework. Thank you for not penalizing him for this. He has a lot on his plate right now, and he is tired today!*

*Sincerely,*
*Parent*


*Dear Parent,*

*Thank you for reaching out and letting me know that Jake is juggling a lot of things at once—it is helpful to know this as his teacher. I have noticed that he has been especially tired in class.*

*I strongly encourage my students to participate in extracurricular activities, and I know that Jake has true athletic talent. Juggling academics and practice is a challenge for all of our athletes, and I know that Coach talks to the team often about the importance of being scholar athletes. As you can imagine, all of our students who are participating in activities would like to forgo homework on the nights that they have practice. Unfortunately, this is not possible; however, I would love to sit down with Jake during lunch tomorrow and help him with organization and time management. Even with his practice schedule, I think that I will be able to help him get back on track. I do not think that this is an issue of the work being too hard, but if I am wrong about that, please let me know.*

*Thank you for reaching out and for your understanding! I will be cheering for Jake at Friday's game!*

*Best,*
*Teacher*

## TALK TO ME

*Dear Administrator,*

*My child is being bullied on the bus, and I am extremely upset about it. He cries every morning before leaving for school, and I am furious. Please tell me what you plan to do to fix this!*

*Thank you.*
*Parent*


*Dear Parent,*

*Thank you for bringing this to my attention. There is nothing worse than seeing your child hurt, and I am so grateful that you reached out. It would be very helpful to get some additional details from you so that I can fix this situation and ensure that it does not happen again. Are you available to meet on Monday? We do not tolerate bullying of any kind, and I am here to support your child. Please know that we will work with you to rectify this situation. Thank you for reaching out to me so that I can get to the bottom of it! Your child is fortunate to have such a wonderful advocate.*

*Sincerely,*
*Administrator*

*Dear Administrator,*

*I am so upset with Matthew's math teacher. He is completely inept. My child does not understand anything that is going on, and his teacher continues to provide poor instruction. We studied for the test for hours, and he still failed it. Can you please tell me how you are going to fix this problem?*

*Parent*


*Dear Parent,*

*Thank you reaching out. I can tell that you are frustrated, and I appreciate you sharing your concerns so that we can rectify the situation. Have you contacted Mr. Teacher about any of these concerns? Also, has your child been attending his help sessions? I would love to meet with you to find a solution. Are you available for a phone call tomorrow sometime between 2 and 5 p.m.? If not, when would be a good time for you? In the meantime, I will meet with Mr. Teacher to discuss your child's struggles in his class so that we can come up with some strategies to help your child. Thank you again, and I look forward to speaking with you. You are a great parent, and like you, we want to see your child succeed!*

*Sincerely,*
*Administrator*

# TALK TO ME

*Dear Cheer Coach,*

*I have had it. My daughter Kara practiced every day and did everything that was recommended to her, yet she still did not make the cheerleading team. She is devastated, and I am, too. Other students who were not as talented as she is were selected. This is definitely favoritism!*

*Please let me know what you plan to do.*

*Thank you,*
*Parent*


*Dear Parent,*

*Thank you for reaching out to let me know how Kara (and you) are feeling. Your daughter is smart, clever, and so very lovely, and to be quite honest, if likability were a factor in the cheer team selection, Kara would have been selected for sure! One of the hardest parts of having team tryouts is that some children will not make it, and this truly breaks my heart. Please know that we had a team of judges who used a very stringent scoring rubric. I don't know if Kara told you, but unfortunately, she forgot several of the moves during the dance portion. She also neglected to smile during her tryout, and I hate that because her smile lights up the room!*

*If it is okay with you, I will sit down with Kara tomorrow to encourage her and let her know all of the amazing gifts I see within her. Please let her know that even the most talented students suffer setbacks, and it is okay to be sad, but she cannot let this define her. I know that this is painful, but in the end, she will be even stronger and more determined for having experienced this.*

*You are an awesome mother, and I know that when your child's heart breaks, yours does, too; however, please know that your precious daughter will have many more opportunities to shine brightly—she is destined for great things!*

*Blessings,*
*Cheer coach*

# FOR PARENTS

Like teaching, parenting is hard! As we all know, teachers, administrators, and parents should work together as a team; however, emotions can sometimes be a barrier to effective communication. The following emails are samples of what a parent might *want to say* in a situation of confusion or frustration. After each, I have put a sample of what we educators *wish you would say* instead. I shared these samples with our parents at our open house, and it completely transformed the way that our parents send us emails, even when they are feeling overwhelmed.

**What parents sometimes want to say:**

*Dear Teacher,*

*How you gonna assign homework tonight after you had my kid go to that performance event for the school?! You must have lost your ever-lovin' mind. You might not have anything else going on tonight, but it is 10 p.m., and we haven't even eaten dinner yet. And now I have to stay up washing and ironing so that my child's uniform is clean. My child will not have the homework, and she certainly will not get a zero.*

*Sincerely,*
*Parent*

**What we wish you'd say:**

*Dear Teacher,*

*How are you? We are kind of struggling here, and I need your help. My child was asked to perform at the school event tonight, and we are just getting home. We haven't eaten dinner yet, and we are trying to get everything done! I know you work on balancing homework, but tonight has been a rough one. Is there any possibility that you would consider an extension for the students who participated in the event? Thank you for all that you do for my child!*

*Best,*
*Parent*

**What you want to say:**

*Dear Teacher,*

*I. Am. Done. My child said he got a detention for saying, "God bless you." You have got to be kidding me! This is out of bounds and completely ridiculous. I refused to sign the form, and he will not be staying tomorrow.*

*Parent*

**What we wish you'd say:**

*Dear Teacher,*

*I hope you are having a good day! I was hoping you could clarify something for me. My child received a detention in your class today for talking, but he said that it is because he said, "God bless you" when someone sneezed. I feel like there has to be more to the story, so I was hoping you could fill me in on the details.*

*Thank you for your help!*
*Parent*

**What you want to say:**

*Dear Teacher,*

*My child dreads going to your class, and that has got to be why she is failing. She is miserable and unhappy because you are incredibly boring. You even bored me at open house, and I only had to be there for fifteen minutes. You have got to do better.*

*Sincerely,*
*Parent*

**What we wish you would say:**

*Dear Teacher,*

*I hope you are having a great day! I apologize for the late email, but I am writing about my concern for Elise, and I need your advice. Lately she has been very weepy and has expressed anxiety about school. I appreciate all that you do for your students, and I know that you work very hard; however, for some reason, Elise is struggling with your class, and I was hoping you could provide me with some insight. In the past, Elise has been the most successful when she is in an interactive environment. She has relayed that your class has more of a lecture format. Do you also find that? Can you give me some insight into her participation in your class and how I can help her be more successful? If you are available to meet in person, I would love to sit down with you and get some advice.*

*With appreciation,*
*Parent*

# FOR BOOK STUDIES

One of the greatest ways to master the six principles is through discussion and simulations. I encourage you to use *Talk to Me* for a book study with your colleagues. Let me know how it goes—tag me @kimbearden so that I can see the great work that you are doing in your organization!

The following exercise is designed for pairs or groups to implement after reading about the six principles. You can spread out the activity over several sessions using different bullet points, or you can do it all in one meeting.

**Directions**

1. Choose at least one bullet point from each of the six principles below.

2. Write each bullet point that you selected on a separate piece of chart paper, and place each piece of chart paper at a different station around the room.

3. Divide into small groups and rotate to each station. Using markers, jot your group members' input on the paper.

4. Spend five to seven minutes at each station before rotating to the next.

After brainstorming your responses, give participants a few minutes to walk around the room and reflect upon the responses. (You might want to give participants star stickers to place next to points that really resonated with them.)

Come back together as a group and discuss the points/principles that rose to the top as areas of success and as areas of concern.

When you have finished, select two to three areas where you need growth, and devise a plan for how you will be more intentional about using the principles to help you. The plans could be individual or group plans, whatever you feel will be most beneficial.

(Note: This activity has been written for schools, but the language could easily be changed for businesses and organizations to reflect your specific needs.)

### Consideration

- What are possible factors that we should take into consideration when dealing with our students?
- What are possible factors that we should take into consideration when dealing with our parents?
- What are possible factors that we should take into consideration when dealing with each other?

### Motivation

- What should be our motivation when dealing with students with academic struggles?
- What should be our motivation when handling students with difficult behavior?
- What should be our motivation when interacting with challenging parents?
- What should be our motivation when interacting with each other?

### Appreciation

- List all of the things you appreciate about our organization.
- List all of the things you appreciate about our students.
- List all of the things you appreciate about our school's parents.

# TALK TO ME

- List all of the things you appreciate about our coworkers.
- List all of the things you appreciate about the work you do.
- List something you appreciate about the challenges you face.

## Validation

- What are some ways to validate our students?
- What are some ways to validate our parents?
- What are some ways to validate our coworkers?

## Celebration

- How can we better celebrate our successes?
- How should we celebrate our relationships with our students?
- How should we celebrate our relationships with our parents?
- How should we celebrate our relationships with each other?

# SIMULATIONS

Below are some scenarios to role play in order to practice the language of the six principles. You can do these with a partner, or you can have pairs do the role play in front of a larger group. Be sure to debrief and offer suggestions afterward. If you get stuck, refer back to your Six Principles Chart on page 66 for sample language to use.

**Parent Conferences**

1. A parent is very frustrated with her child's lack of progress in your class. You have been working very hard to meet his needs, but he is not completing work at home.

2. A parent is overly protective and does all of her son's work for him. He needs to learn to be more independent, and she needs to stop coddling him.

3. A parent does not like a grade that you gave her child for his project.

4. A parent feels that her child is too advanced for your class and is bored.

5. A parent does not like the consequences that you gave her child for misbehavior.

6. A parent is complaining about other children in the class who she feels get more attention than her child does.

**Student Conferences**

1. A student is not working up to his/her potential, and you want to know why.

2. A student is mistreating classmates and calling them names.

3. A student is being disruptive in your class and is not paying attention during instruction.

4. A student is continuously late to your class, and you want this to change.

5. A student is not acting like himself/herself, and you are concerned.

6. A student is gossiping about others and is causing drama.

**Coworker Interactions**

1. A coworker is constantly taking credit for work that you have done.

2. A coworker often fails to follow through on his or her responsibilities, and you feel like they are passed on to you.

3. You sense that a coworker is talking badly about you for no good reason.

4. A coworker complains about everyone and everything, and it is making the environment toxic.

5. A coworker seems very upset and stressed.

6. A coworker is having a hard time doing an effective job and lacks skills.

# ACKNOWLEDGMENTS

**To my husband, Scotty:** You are my rock and my calm in the storm. Thank you for always believing in me and supporting me. You still make me weak in the knees, and my love for you is endless.

**To my daughter, Madison:** I am so proud of the extraordinary woman you have become. You are love and light; you are forever my baby girl. I love you beyond measure.

**To my sons, Sisipho, Sabelo, and Phakamani:** You are a precious gift to me and to this world, and you have filled our lives with incomprehensible joy. I am so blessed and grateful to be your mother, and I cannot wait to see how God's divine plan continues to unfold. I love you more than words can express.

**To my daddy, Jack Driscoll:** You are the one who taught me the meaning of unconditional love. You are the world's best daddy, and I love you so very much. Thank you for always believing in me.

**To my precious mother in heaven:** I love and miss you so much, Mama. I hope that I continue to make you proud.

**To my brothers, Bobby and Stephen Driscoll:** It is wonderful to know that no matter what happens in life, you will always have my back. You taught me to be fierce and strong. I love you.

**To my son-in-law, Taylor Hunt:** Long before I knew you, I prayed for the man my daughter would marry one day. Thank you for exceeding everything I ever hoped for. You are such a blessing to our family.

**To the phenomenal staff of the Ron Clark Academy:**

| | | |
|---|---|---|
| Kenneth Adams | Pamela Haskins | David Spearman |
| Jeffrey J. Amezqua | Dr. Camille Jones | Jai Springs |
| Susan Barnes | Dasia Kirkley | Daniel Thompson |
| Joey Barr | Hope King | Elektra Thompson |
| Junior Bernadin | Wade King | Alejandro Uria |
| Kirk Brown | Rhonda Lokey | Kyle Walcott |
| Renita Burns | Hutch McMillan | Carrie-Jo Wallace |
| Nadia Chochol | Tully Murray | Benjamin Walker |
| Ron Clark | Chrissi Pepitone | Aungelita Williams |
| Korey Collins | Aujahuna Smith | Jordan Jones Wright |

... and all those who came before you. I am so grateful to call you my family. Thank you for your love, laughter, hard work, and dedication. You are extraordinary human beings, and you inspire me to do more, be more, and give more each and every day. I love you.

**To J. Amezqua:** Thank you for taking the photos for this book at a moment's notice and for capturing so many of RCA's most precious memories with your camera lens. You are a genius, and we are so grateful to have you as a part of our family.

**To Todd Nesloney:** Thank you for giving me the perfect title for this book and for being a constant sounding board. I am blessed to call you friend.

**To the Board of Trustees of the Ron Clark Academy:** Thank you for sharing your time, talents, and resources with us. Your dedication and support help us transform countless lives, and I am forever grateful.

**To Duane Ward, Ryan Giffen, and the rest of the team at Premiere Speakers Bureau:** It has been an honor to be represented by you for the past seventeen years. Thank you for providing me with the privilege to speak to thousands of educators around the world. I greatly appreciate all that you have done for RCA and for me.

**To Dave and Shelley Burgess:** Thank you for giving educators a voice so that we can work together to change the world.

**To my amazing, beloved students, past and present:** You have blessed me beyond measure, and you give my life purpose. I am better because of you, and I love you all.

**To the past and present parents of RCA, especially my beloved mamas:** In some ways, this book was written as a love letter to you. Thank you for trusting me, sharing your hearts with me, and believing in me. My admiration for you and your hard work is endless. You make me a better woman, a better mother, a better teacher, and a better human being.

**And to Ron Clark:** I cannot imagine my life without you, for you showed me my life's purpose. You could have chosen anyone to cofound the school with you, yet you chose me. I love you, my precious friend. The best is yet to come.

# ABOUT THE RON CLARK ACADEMY

The Ron Clark Academy (RCA) is a highly acclaimed, nonprofit middle school in Atlanta that promotes innovation and engages its students through energetic teaching balanced by a strict code of discipline. Each year, thousands of educators from around the world participate in RCA's staff development training, the RCA Experience, to learn how to replicate the school's style, philosophy, and success in their own schools.

While at RCA, participants have the opportunity to observe master teachers instructing classes of children with various levels of academic, social, and emotional development. In addition to classroom observations, educators also attend workshops throughout the course of the day. A focus is placed on showing educators how to increase student engagement, promote academic rigor, and create a climate and culture for student success. To learn more about the RCA Experience, please visit ronclarkacademy.com.

# MORE FROM

# DAVE BURGESS
## Consulting, Inc.

### Teach Like a PIRATE
*Increase Student Engagement, Boost Your Creativity, and Transform Your Life as an Educator*
By Dave Burgess (@BurgessDave)

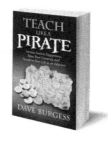

*New York Times'* bestseller *Teach Like a PIRATE* sparked a worldwide educational revolution with its passionate teaching manifesto and dynamic student-engagement strategies. Translated into multiple languages, it sparks outrageously creative lessons and life-changing student experiences.

### P is for PIRATE
*Inspirational ABCs for Educators*
By Dave and Shelley Burgess (@Burgess_Shelley)

In *P is for Pirate*, husband-and-wife team Dave and Shelley Burgess tap personal experiences of seventy educators to inspire others to create fun and exciting places to learn. It's a wealth of imaginative and creative ideas that makes learning and teaching more fulfilling than ever before.

### The Innovator's Mindset
*Empower Learning, Unleash Talent, and Lead a Culture of Creativity*
By George Couros (@gcouros)

In *The Innovator's Mindset*, teachers and administrators discover that compliance to a scheduled curriculum hinders student innovation, critical thinking, and creativity. To become forward-thinking leaders, students must be empowered to wonder and explore.

### Pure Genius
*Building a Culture of Innovation and Taking 20% Time
to the Next Level*
By Don Wettrick (@DonWettrick)

Collaboration—with experts, students, and other educators—helps create interesting and even life-changing opportunities for learning. In *Pure Genius*, Don Wettrick inspires and equips educators with a systematic blueprint for beating classroom boredom and teaching innovation.

### Learn Like a PIRATE
*Empower Your Students to Collaborate, Lead,
and Succeed*
By Paul Solarz (@PaulSolarz)

Passing grades don't equip students for life and career responsibilities. *Learn Like a PIRATE* shows how risk-taking and exploring passions in stimulating, motivating, supportive, self-directed classrooms creates students capable of making smart, responsible decisions on their own.

### Ditch That Textbook
*Free Your Teaching and Revolutionize Your Classroom*
By Matt Miller (@jmattmiller)

*Ditch That Textbook* creates a support system, toolbox, and manifesto that can free teachers from outdated textbooks. Miller empowers them to untether themselves, throw out meaningless, pedestrian teaching and learning practices, and evolve and revolutionize their classrooms.

### Lead Like a PIRATE
*Make School Amazing for Your Students and Staff*
By Shelley Burgess and Beth Houf
(@Burgess_Shelley, @BethHouf)

*Lead Like a PIRATE* maps out character traits necessary to captain a school or district. You'll learn where to find treasure already in your classrooms and schools—and bring out the best in educators. Find encouragement in your relentless quest to make school amazing for everyone!

### 50 Things You Can Do with Google Classroom
By Alice Keeler and Libbi Miller
(@alicekeeler, @MillerLibbi)

*50 Things You Can Do with Google Classroom* provides a thorough overview of this GAfE app and shortens the teacher learning curve for introducing technology in the classroom. Keeler and Miller's ideas, instruction, and screenshots help teachers go digital with this powerful tool.

### 50 Things to Go Further with Google Classroom
*A Student-Centered Approach*
By Alice Keeler and Libbi Miller
(@alicekeeler, @MillerLibbi)

In *50 Things to Go Further with Google Classroom: A Student-Centered Approach*, authors and educators Alice Keeler and Libbi Miller help teachers create a digitally rich, engaging, student-centered environment that taps the power of individualized learning using Google Classroom.

### 140 Twitter Tips for Educators
*Get Connected, Grow Your Professional Learning Network, and Reinvigorate Your Career*
By Brad Currie, Billy Krakower, and Scott Rocco
(@bradmcurrie, @wkrakower, @ScottRRocco)

In *140 Twitter Tips for Educators*, #Satchat hosts and founders of Evolving Educators, Brad Currie, Billy Krakower, and Scott Rocco, offer step-by-step instruction on Twitter basics and building an online following within Twitter's vibrant network of educational professionals.

### Master the Media
*How Teaching Media Literacy Can Save Our Plugged-In World*
By Julie Smith (@julnilsmith)

*Master the Media* explains media history, purpose, and messaging so teachers and parents can empower students with critical-thinking skills which lead to informed choices, the ability to differentiate between truth and lies, and discern perception from reality. Media literacy can save the world.

### The Zen Teacher
*Creating Focus, Simplicity, and Tranquility in the Classroom*
By Dan Tricarico (@thezenteacher)

Unrushed and fully focused, teachers influence—even improve—the future when they maximize performance and improve their quality of life. In *The Zen Teacher*, Dan Tricarico offers practical, easy-to-use techniques to develop a non-religious Zen practice and thrive in the classroom.

### eXPlore Like a Pirate
*Gamification and Game-Inspired Course Design to Engage, Enrich, and Elevate Your Learners*
By Michael Matera (@MrMatera)

Create an experiential, collaborative, and creative world with classroom game designer and educator Michael Matera's game-based learning book, *eXPlore Like a Pirate*. Matera helps teachers apply motivational gameplay techniques and enhance curriculum with gamification strategies.

### Your School Rocks . . . So Tell People!
*Passionately Pitch and Promote the Positives Happening on Your Campus*
By Ryan McLane and Eric Lowe
(@McLane_Ryan, @EricLowe21)

*Your School Rocks . . . So Tell People!* helps schools create effective social media communication strategies that keep students' families and the community connected to what's going on at school, offering more than seventy immediately actionable tips with easy-to-follow instructions and video tutorial links.

### Play Like a Pirate
*Engage Students with Toys, Games, and Comics*
By Quinn Rollins (@jedikermit)

In *Play Like a Pirate*, Quinn Rollins offers practical, engaging strategies and resources that make it easy to integrate fun into your curriculum. Regardless of grade level, serious learning can be seriously fun with inspirational ideas that engage students in unforgettable ways.

### The Classroom Chef
*Sharpen Your Lessons. Season Your Classes. Make Math Meaningful*
By John Stevens and Matt Vaudrey
(@Jstevens009, @MrVaudrey)

With imagination and preparation, every teacher can be *The Classroom Chef* using John Stevens and Matt Vaudrey's secret recipes, ingredients, and tips that help students "get" math. Use ideas as-is, or tweak to create enticing educational meals that engage students.

### How Much Water Do We Have?
*5 Success Principles for Conquering Any Challenge and Thriving in Times of Change*
By Pete Nunweiler with Kris Nunweiler

Stressed out, overwhelmed, or uncertain at work or home? It could be figurative dehydration.
*How Much Water Do We Have?* identifies five key elements necessary for success of any goal, life transition, or challenge. Learn to find, acquire, and use the 5 Waters of Success.

### The Writing on the Classroom Wall
*How Posting Your Most Passionate Beliefs about Education Can Empower Your Students, Propel Your Growth, and Lead to a Lifetime of Learning*
By Steve Wyborney (@SteveWyborney)

Big ideas lead to deeper learning, but they don't have to be profound to have profound impact. Teacher Steve Wyborney explains why and how sharing ideas sharpens and refines them. It's okay if some ideas fall off the wall; what matters most is sharing and discussing.

### Kids Deserve It!
*Pushing Boundaries and Challenging Conventional Thinking*
By Todd Nesloney and Adam Welcome
(@TechNinjaTodd, @awelcome)

Think big. Make learning fun and meaningful. *Kids Deserve It!* Nesloney and Welcome offer high-tech, high-touch, and highly engaging practices that inspire risk-taking and shake up the status quo on behalf of your students. Rediscover why you became an educator, too!

### LAUNCH
*Using Design Thinking to Boost Creativity and Bring Out the Maker in Every Student*
By John Spencer and A.J. Juliani
(@spencerideas, @ajjuliani)

When students identify themselves as makers, inventors, and creators, they discover powerful problem-solving and critical-thinking skills. Their imaginations and creativity will shape our future. John Spencer and A.J. Juliani's *LAUNCH* process dares you to innovate and empower them.

### Instant Relevance
*Using Today's Experiences to Teach Tomorrow's Lessons*
By Denis Sheeran (@MathDenisNJ)

Learning sticks when it's relevant to students. In *Instant Relevance*, author and keynote speaker Denis Sheeran equips you to create engaging lessons from experiences and events that matter to students while helping them make meaningful connections between the real world and the classroom.

### Escaping the School Leader's Dunk Tank
*How to Prevail When Others Want to See You Drown*
By Rebecca Coda and Rick Jetter
(@RebeccaCoda, @RickJetter)

Dunk-tank situations—discrimination, bad politics, revenge, or ego-driven coworkers—can make an educator's life miserable. Coda and Jetter (dunk-tank survivors themselves) share real-life stories and insightful research to equip school leaders with tools to survive and, better yet, avoid getting "dunked."

### Start. Right. Now.
*Teach and Lead for Excellence*
By Todd Whitaker, Jeff Zoul, and Jimmy Casas
(@ToddWhitaker, @Jeff_Zoul, @casas_jimmy)

Excellent leaders and teachers Know the Way, Show the Way, Go the Way, and Grow Each Day. Whitaker, Zoul, and Casas share four key behaviors of excellence from educators across the U.S. and motivate to put you on the right path.

### Teaching Math with Google Apps
*50 G Suite Activities*
By Alice Keeler and Diana Herrington
(@AliceKeeler, @mathdiana)

*Teaching Math with Google Apps* meshes the easy student/teacher interaction of Google Apps with G Suite that empowers student creativity and critical thinking. Keeler and Herrington demonstrate fifty ways to bring math classes into the twenty-first century with easy-to-use technology.

### Table Talk Math
*A Practical Guide for Bringing Math into Everyday Conversations*
By John Stevens (@Jstevens009)

In *Table Talk Math*, John Stevens offers parents—and teachers—ideas for initiating authentic, math-based, everyday conversations that get kids to notice and pique their curiosity about the numbers, patterns, and equations in the world around them.

### Shift This!
*How to Implement Gradual Change for Massive Impact in Your Classroom*
By Joy Kirr (@JoyKirr)

Establishing a student-led culture focused on individual responsibility and personalized learning is possible, sustainable, and even easy when it happens little by little. In *Shift This!*, Joy Kirr details gradual shifts in thinking, teaching, and approach for massive impact in your classroom.

### Unmapped Potential
*An Educator's Guide to Lasting Change*
By Julie Hasson and Missy Lennard (@PPrincipals)

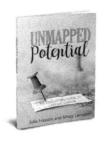

Overwhelmed and overworked? You're not alone, but it can get better. You simply need the right map to guide you from frustrated to fulfilled. *Unmapped Potential* offers advice and practical strategies to forge a unique path to becoming the educator and person you want to be.

### Shattering the Perfect Teacher Myth
*6 Truths That Will Help You THRIVE as an Educator*
By Aaron Hogan (@aaron_hogan)

Author and educator Aaron Hogan helps shatter the idyllic "perfect teacher" myth, which erodes self-confidence with unrealistic expectations and sets teachers up for failure. His book equips educators with strategies that help them shift out of survival mode and THRIVE.

### Social LEADia
*Moving Students from Digital Citizenship to Digital Leadership*
By Jennifer Casa-Todd (@JCasaTodd)

A networked society requires students to leverage social media to connect to people, passions, and opportunities to grow and make a difference. *Social LEADia* helps shift focus at school and home from digital citizenship to digital leadership and equip students for the future.

### Spark Learning
*3 Keys to Embracing the Power of Student Curiosity*
By Ramsey Musallam (@ramusallam)

Inspired by his popular TED Talk "3 Rules to Spark Learning," Musallam combines brain science research, proven teaching methods, and his personal story to empower you to improve your students' learning experiences by inspiring inquiry and harnessing its benefits.

### Ditch That Homework
*Practical Strategies to Help Make Homework Obsolete*
By Matt Miller and Alice Keeler
(@jmattmiller, @alicekeeler)

In *Ditch That Homework*, Miller and Keeler discuss the pros and cons of homework, why it's assigned, and what life could look like without it. They evaluate research, share parent and teacher insights, then make a convincing case for ditching it for effective and personalized learning methods.

### The Four O'Clock Faculty
*A Rogue Guide to Revolutionizing Professional Development*
By Rich Czyz (@RACzyz)

In *The Four O'Clock Faculty*, Rich identifies ways to make professional learning meaningful, efficient, and, above all, personally relevant. It's a practical guide to revolutionize PD, revealing why some is so awful and what you can do to change the model for the betterment of everyone.

### Culturize
*Every Student. Every Day. Whatever It Takes.*
By Jimmy Casas (@casas_jimmy)

*Culturize* dives into what it takes to cultivate a community of learners who embody innately human traits our world desperately needs—kindness, honesty, and compassion. Casas's stories reveal how "soft skills" can be honed while exceeding academic standards of twenty-first-century learning.

### Code Breaker
*Increase Creativity, Remix Assessment, and Develop a Class of Coder Ninjas!*
By Brian Aspinall (@mraspinall)

You don't have to be a "computer geek" to use coding to turn curriculum expectations into student skills. Use *Code Breaker* to teach students how to identify problems, develop solutions, and use computational thinking to apply and demonstrate learning.

### The Wild Card
*7 Steps to an Educator's Creative Breakthrough*
By Hope and Wade King
(@hopekingteach, @wadeking7)

The Kings facilitate a creative breakthrough in the classroom with *The Wild Card*, a step-by-step guide to drawing on your authentic self to deliver your content creatively and be the wild card who changes the game for your learners.

### Stories from Webb
*The Ideas, Passions, and Convictions of a Principal and His School Family*
By Todd Nesloney (@TechNinjaTodd)

*Stories from Webb* goes right to the heart of education. Told by award-winning principal Todd Nesloney and his dedicated team of staff and teachers, this book reminds you why you became an educator. Relatable stories reinvigorate and may inspire you to tell your own!

### The Principled Principal
*10 Principles for Leading Exceptional Schools*
By Jeffrey Zoul and Anthony McConnell
(@Jeff_Zoul, @mcconnellaw)

Zoul and McConnell know from personal experience that the role of school principal is one of the most challenging and the most rewarding in education. Using relatable stories and real-life examples, they reveal ten core values that will empower you to work and lead with excellence.

### The Limitless School
*Creative Ways to Solve the Culture Puzzle*
By Abe Hege and Adam Dovico
(@abehege, @adamdovico)

Being intentional about creating a positive culture is imperative for your school's success. This book identifies the nine pillars that support a positive school culture and explains how each stakeholder has a vital role to play in the work of making schools safe, inviting, and dynamic.

### Google Apps for Littles
*Believe They Can*
By Christine Pinto and Alice Keeler
(@PintoBeanz11, @alicekeeler)

Learn how to tap into students' natural curiosity using technology. Pinto and Keeler share a wealth of innovative ways to integrate digital tools in the primary classroom to make learning engaging and relevant for even the youngest of today's twenty-first-century learners.

### Be the One for Kids
*You Have the Power to Change the Life of a Child*

By Ryan Sheehy (@sheehyrw)

Students need guidance to succeed academically, but they also need our help to survive and thrive in today's turbulent world. They need someone to model the attributes that will help them win not just in school but in life as well. That someone is you.

### Let Them Speak
*How Student Voice Can Transform Your School*
By Rebecca Coda and Rick Jetter
(@RebeccaCoda, @RickJetter)

We say, "Student voice matters," but are we really listening? This book will inspire you to find out what your students really think, feel, and need. You'll learn how to listen to and use student feedback to improve your school's culture. All you have to do is ask—and then *Let Them Speak*.

### The EduProtocol Field Guide
*16 Student-Centered Lesson Frames for Infinite Learning Possibilities*
By Marlena Hebern and Jon Corippo
(@mhebern, @jcorippo)

Are you ready to break out of the lesson-and-worksheet rut? Use *The EduProtocol Field Guide* to create engaging and effective instruction, build culture, and deliver content to K–12 students in a supportive, creative environment.

### All 4s and 5s
*A Guide to Teaching and Leading Advanced Placement Programs*

Andrew Sharos (@AndrewSharosAP)

AP classes shouldn't be relegated to "privileged" schools and students. With proper support, every student can experience success. *All 4s and 5s* offers a wealth of classroom and program strategies that equip you to develop a culture of academic and personal excellence.

### Shake Up Learning
*Practical Ideas to Move Learning from Static to Dynamic*

By Kasey Bell (@ShakeUpLearning)

Is the learning in your classroom static or dynamic? *Shake Up Learning* guides you through the process of creating dynamic learning opportunities—from purposeful planning and maximizing technology to fearless implementation.

### The Secret Solution
*How One Principal Discovered the Path to Success*

Todd Whitaker, Sam Miller, and Ryan Donlan (@ToddWhitaker, @SamMiller29, @RyanDonlan)

This entertaining parable provides leaders with a non-threatening tool to discuss problematic attitudes in schools. In the updated edition, you'll find a reader's guide to help you identify habits and traits that can propel you and your team to success.

### The Path to Serendipity
*Discover the Gifts along Life's Journey*

By Allyson Apsey (@AllysonApsey)

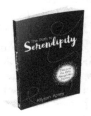

In this funny, genuine, and clever book, Allyson Apsey shares relatable stories and practical strategies for living a meaningful life regardless of the craziness happening around you. You'll discover that you really do have the power to choose the kind of life you live—every day.

### Lead with Culture
*What Really Matters in Our Schools*

By Jay Billy (@JayBilly2)

In this *Lead Like a PIRATE Guide*, Jay Billy explains that making school a place where students and staff want to be starts with culture. You'll be inspired by this principal's practical ideas for creating a sense of unity—even in the most diverse communities.

### Sparks in the Dark
*Lessons, Ideas, and Strategies to Illuminate the*
*Reading and Writing Lives in All of Us*
By Travis Crowder and Todd Nesloney
(@teachermantrav, @TechNinjaTodd)

More standards, tests, and mandates are not the answer to improving literacy. *Sparks in the Dark* inspires educators in every subject area to be intentional about instilling a love of reading and writing in all students.

### The Pepper Effect
*Tap into the Magic of Creativity, Collaboration, and Innovation*
By Sean Gaillard (@smgaillard)

Using *Sgt. Pepper's Lonely Hearts Club Band* by The Beatles as a template for inspiration, Sean Gaillard explores the necessary steps for creating the conditions for motivation, collaboration, creativity, and innovation in your schoolhouse.

### The EduNinja Mindset
*11 Habits for Building a Stronger Mind and Body*
By Jennifer Burdis (@jennifer_burdis)

As a two-time American Ninja Warrior contestant, educator, and trainer, Jen Burdis pushes herself to physically and mentally overcome obstacles. In *The EduNinja Mindset*, Burdis shares her strategies to empower teachers, students and families to develop healthy habits.

### Be REAL
*Educate from the Heart*
By Tara Martin (@TaraMartinEDU)

REAL educators are relatable, they expose vulnerability by sharing their experiences, they are approachable, they learn through life. They are the heart of our schools. In *Be REAL*, you'll learn the power of being true to yourself and find the courage to teach from the heart.

# ABOUT THE AUTHOR

**Kim Bearden** is the cofounder, executive director, and language arts teacher at the highly acclaimed Ron Clark Academy, an innovative middle school and educator-training facility in Atlanta. More than fifty thousand educators from around the world have visited Kim's classroom and have attended her workshops to learn better ways to engage students, promote academic rigor, and create a climate and culture that promote success.

In 2016, Kim was honored at the White House for being inducted into to the National Teachers Hall of Fame. She is the recipient of the Disney American Teacher Award for Humanities and the Milken Family Foundation Award for Excellence in Education. She was chosen to receive the InfluencHer Award, the University of Georgia Outstanding Educator Award, and the Turknett Character Award for Servant Leadership. Women Works Media Group named her one of Georgia's Most Powerful and Influential Women.

Over the past thirty-one years, she has been a teacher, instructional lead teacher, curriculum director, school board member, staff development trainer, and middle school principal. Kim's first book, *Crash Course: The Life Lessons My Students Taught Me*, made several bestseller lists.

Kim resides in a suburb of Atlanta with her husband, Scotty, and her three sons, Sisipho, Sabelo, and Phakamani. Her married daughter, Madison, lives close by.

To learn more about Kim,
Follow her on Instagram, Twitter,
and Facebook @kimbearden.
or
Visit her website at
kimbearden.com.

To book Kim to speak at your
next event, contact
Premiere Speakers Bureau:
premierespeakers.com.

CPSIA information can be obtained
at www.ICGtesting.com
Printed in the USA
LVHW051231220723
753115LV00006B/115